Change Your Life With Humor

Create a Happier, Healthier and FUNNIER --- YOU!

Dr. Lorrie Boyd
Lola Gillebaard
Stewart and Jeanne Lerner

Change Your Life With Humor

Create a Happier, Healthier, and Funnier -- YOU!

by

Lorrie Boyd
Lola Gillebaard
Stewart & Jeanne Lerner

Copyright c 1993 by Lorrie Boyd, Lola Gillebaard, Stewart Lerner, and Jeanne Lerner.

First printing 1993.   10 9 8 7 6 5 4 3 2 1

Type-set by ADD/WRITE, Long Beach, CA 90815 (310 421-4184)

Cover by Mike CapDeVille, Long Beach, CA 90803

Full-page illustrations by James Silvani. All rights reserved.

All other graphic art c 1992 Epyx, Inc., Box 8020, Redwood City, CA 94063. All rights reserved.

Publisher's Cataloging in Publication Data
Change your life with humor: Create a healthier, happier, and funnier -- YOU! / by Lorrie Boyd, Lola Gillebaard, Stewart Lerner, & Jeanne Lerner
p. cm.
1. Wit and humor--Therapeutic use.   2. Self-realization.   I. Boyd, Lorrie.
BF575.L3C52 1993   152.4   QBI92-20350
Library of Congress Catalog Card Number 92-75523
ISBN 0-9635133-0-3: $14.95 Softcover

DEDICATION

For my parents, who taught me **why**;
For my husband, who taught me **how**;
For my kids, who taught me **when**.

-- Lola

For all the teachers
who made me laugh
while they taught me
how to speak and write.

-- Jeanne

To my parents, who always told me
there was nothing I could not do.

-- Stewart

To my grandmothers, Reta Bennett and
Betty Albert, who filled my life with
love, laughter, and playfulness.

-- Lorrie

Table of Contents

Introduction

Like a powerful mood-elevating drug, humor lifts our spirits and improves our sense of well-being. Humor is a tranquilizer which is addictive because of the good feelings it creates both emotionally and physically.

If a body hasn't laughed in a while, it goes through withdrawal similar to the changes one goes through during "cold turkey" abstinence or dieting. When our bodies experience these changes, we become irritable, impatient and intolerant. Without humor in our lives, we become sour and unfriendly grouches.

Humor is much like beauty, in that humor is in the eye and the funnybone of the beholder. Therefore, we are all limited by the fact that humor is personal.

When we began this book, we looked up "humor" in the dictionary, and the entry read, "Anything funny." We weren't quite sure what that meant so we looked up "funny." It said, "See humor." With that specific answer in mind, we began the arduous task of writing about something almost as concrete as smoke.

Webster's *New World Dictionary* defines humor as "a state of mind." If we are in an open frame of mind and are willing to "find" humor and to let it find us, then almost anything can be perceived as humorous.

The authors of this book strongly believe that humor, used properly, can create many positive changes in our lives. Humor is a breath of fresh air, a ray of sunshine, a glimmer of hope. A laugh can brighten your day, change your mood, and positively impact illness and disease.

To some degree, we all have discovered the powerful effects of humor. Whether we use it to soften the devastating blows of divorce or crippling illness, or to ease such day-to-day crises as nagging bosses, frustrating traffic, and those neck pains caused by those pain-in-the-neck people, we are protecting ourselves from emotional or physical collapse. Through trial and error we have discovered that laughing at our predicaments seems to lessen their severity.

Humor can help to make us more productive by infusing enthusiasm and fun into our work habits. These are great swords to combat complacency and boredom. Humor can inspire us to achieve feats that previously we would not have considered possible.

The more we laugh, the better we feel about ourselves and the people around us. This helps us to project a feeling of contentment and confidence.

All around us, we will find people who are in great need of humor. Indeed, they want very much to laugh but have either forgotten how or it has been so long since they laughed that they no longer believe they can. We can help these people because humor is very contagious.

As we look on the lighter side and share our laughter, we reach out and touch the lives of those who need laughter to lighten their loads. As they laugh with us, they will learn to laugh at themselves. A bond of laughter is forged, upon which friendship can grow.

There are those who feel they do not have time to laugh. Others feel that they laugh enough, when, in fact, the last time they really laughed, Ronald Reagan had only one wrinkle. These people may be taking life too seriously and need to slow down and ease up.

> There is more to life than increasing its
> speed.
> -- Mohandas K. Gandhi

Unfortunately, they might learn the hard way when they get hauled away to the hospital for hypertension or other stress-related ailments.

Do your feet ever get sore? People who have walked long distances, waited in line for hours, or stood on their feet all day know how sore their feet can get. This is natural because our feet are not designed to be in constant use. They need a break.

The rest of our body functions in the same way. Unless we give our body a break, it too will refuse to function. The collapse is usually far more gradual and is preceded by subtle warning signals. The first warnings may be frequent headaches or other pains, because the brain is screaming for a break. For many, the first inclination is to drop a few pills or use the sedative effect of alcohol.

Unfortunately, these are not healthy solutions. We are simply numbing that area of the brain so that it <u>feels</u> like the pressure is gone, when, in fact, we just can't feel it anymore. Eventually, we may end up chewing pills like candy or be well on our way to a serious problem with alcohol.

In either case, the aches still occur. There is a much simpler (and healthier) remedy for these aches and pains.

Learn to laugh. Take a humor break. Your brain will thank you by relaxing those muscles which have been gripping your head, the result: fewer aches and pains.

Contained in this book are the tools you will need to effectively use humor in all parts of your life. For easy use, our book is organized in three sections:

Section One provides some brief background information on humor. It illustrates an historical perspective and discusses the psychological and physiological benefits of humor.

Section Two discusses in more detail how humor can be used to enrich your life in a variety of different areas. Insights and techniques illustrate how you can use humor to enhance your overall lifestyle and even deal with grief or loss.

Section Three shares secrets of humor and provides you with a workbook that will give you ideas, techniques, and tools to "tickle your funny bone."

Welcome to the wonderful world of humor. Read and enjoy!

The new and improved me!

ONE

The History
and Effects
of Humor

1

History of Humor

*"You can't really be strong until you see the
funny side of things."*

-- Ken Kesey

Throughout the ages, many writers have
observed and described the beneficial effects of
humor. Not only did they find that it was
enjoyable, but some went so far as to suggest
that it was vital to human survival.

As early as ancient Greece, laughter has
been recommended as a strategy for improving
man's health and well-being. Although the Greek
theater is famous for its tragedies, comedies also
commanded huge audiences because of their
power to relax and relieve ancient Athenians of
their daily stresses. Menander, considered the
foremost author of Greek comedies, used slapstick to entertain his audiences, relieving their
tensions.

Roman playwrights were also involved in the
creation of humorous theatrical offerings. Farce
was a favorite fare of Roman theater goers. The
modern musical play, "A Funny Thing Happened

on the Way to the Forum," satirizes the ancient Roman comedies and entertains audiences with its heavy-handed humor. The Roman writer, Seneca, stated, "All things are cause either for laughter or weeping." As a society, Romans preferred to laugh.

Historians of the Middle Ages have recorded that doctors of that time tended to connect human emotions with body organs. They believed that love was an emotion of the heart, while laughter was linked to the spleen. Christian society of that time deemed humor unbefitting to man's spiritual life. However, many morality plays of those times did use humor to illustrate man's tendency to sinful excesses.

The Seven Deadly Sins were brought to life through humorous examples. Early Christians believed that recreation, sports, games, plays, and comedies were immoral. They also made them illegal in some Christian countries. This attitude was repeated in the founding Pilgrim fathers, who scorned laughter unless it was being used to illuminate a moral lesson.

In Shakespeare's time, wit meant knowledge or sophistication, but the favorite form of humor was still slapstick. His comedies contained visual jokes as well as bawdy sexual references. Double meanings with sexual references were frequent; but since Elizabethan audiences were unsophisticated in humor, there is little record of satire.

The mannered society of France nurtured the art of farce. Comedies of manners and bedroom farces were the favorites of 18th century France. The double entendre was in full flower. French farces are popular even today and currently show on Broadway.

Nineteenth century writer Herbert Spencer was one of those who recommended that laughter might be useful to man. He wrote that it was a mechanism for releasing excess tension. For this reason he concluded that it was an important restorative mechanism.

Sigmund Freud studied human emotions and their effect on the human body. In his examinations, he found that hostility, aggression, and bitterness were frequently linked to negative humor. On the other hand, he concluded that there were definite positive effects of humor, such as liberation of the emotions and elevation of pleasurable feelings.

This reflection suggests the difference between laughing AT someone and laughing

WITH someone. Freud also asserted that laughter arises when psychic energy is freed from its more or less static function of repressing the forbidden thought.

The freedom from repression and the freedom of thought provide an enjoyable shock which produces delighted laughter. Freud clearly was an advocate of the positive benefits of humor.

The literature of America is full of wonderful examples of humorous writing. Mark Twain made folksy satire popular. He exaggerated everyday happenings to help his readers see the humor of life.

James Thurber and Ring Lardner chose the same style of wit and satire at a later time. Thurber's character, Walter Mitty, has come to represent all hen-pecked husbands with dreams of freedom and glory.

Will Rogers delighted audiences with his rope twirling and his down-home, political satire. No institution or political office holder was safe from the barbs of his lampoons. He became the confidant of congressmen and cabinet officers by poking fun at them. And yet, he never took himself too seriously, as evidenced by this quote: "I don't make jokes. I just watch the government and report the facts."

Modern political satire owes a debt to this free thinking cowboy who pointed out the weaknesses of American politicians to the delight of their constituents.

Contemporary philosopher Norman Cousins ascribed miraculous healing powers to humor and laughter. His work, *Anatomy of an Illness*, describes his use of humor in a battle with an illness which had been diagnosed as terminal. Cousins became a professor at UCLA medical school as a result of this work with humor therapy.

Today's popular humor is frequently viewed as television situation comedy. Many adults have been nurtured and relaxed with the comedic view of life pictured on "The Bill Cosby Show." Subtle satire has given way to the more obvious humor of "Saturday Night Live."

History has taught us that, in whatever format it is cloaked, humor provides us with an escape from our real-world existence--a healthy release from stress and tension. And, hopefully, it brings out the child in us. As Woody Allen has stated, "Humorists always sit at the children's table."

2

Physiological Effects of Humor

The art of medicine consists of amusing the patient while nature cures the disease.

-- Voltaire

Although researchers have not thoroughly documented that "laughter is the best medicine," immunologist Lee Burk has increased evidence that humor positively affects our immune system.

In addition, Dr. William Fry of Stanford University has documented that laughter creates a cardiovascular and nervous system reaction which stimulates a chemical reaction which produces endorphins, a morphine-like pain-reducing enzyme.

The research that exists in this field all demonstrates that there ARE physical benefits to humor. Our physical well-being may in fact be directly linked to the amount of humor we encounter in the process of our lives.

Norman Cousins, former editor of the *Saturday Review* magazine and author, was mentioned in the chapter on the history of humor. Upon returning from a particularly stressful trip abroad, he was diagnosed as suffering from a serious collagen disease. This life-threatening disease disintegrates the connective tissue of the spine. The disease caused him great pain and difficulty in moving.

Cousins convinced his doctor to allow him to take control of part of his own treatment. He used humor as a therapeutic aid to his recovery.

Cousins checked himself into the more cheerful atmosphere of a luxury hotel and proceeded to create his own daily program for recovery. This program combined viewing Marx Brothers films and reruns of the television hit, "Candid Camera." A nutritious diet and large doses of Vitamin C were also part of his regimen. Luckily for future students of humor and recovery, Cousins documented his progress.

Cousins discovered that after each ten-minute period of hearty belly laughter, he would sleep for one hour pain-free. A permanent reduction of inflammation was also attributed to sessions of laughter. Cousins used laughter to create a mood which was conducive to the use of other positive emotions to heal.

These same endorphins are produced during vigorous exercise. Many joggers and long-distance runners experience a feeling of euphoria which is known as the "runner's high."

As stated earlier, laughter can reduce pain.
Humor may not totally eradicate pain, but it can
help us to gain control over it. When we pay
attention to pain, it intensifies. Humor distracts
us from the aches and pains of such diseases as
arthritis and rheumatism. When we are laughing, we don't notice the source of physical dis-
comfort.

Specific physiological reactions occur in our
bodies when we laugh. These include exercise for
the lungs, stimulation of the circulatory system,
and full action of the diaphragm. The deep
breathing which accompanies laughter benefits
the cardiovascular system because it increases
oxygen in the blood. Even someone who has
been inactive due to long-term or seriously
debilitating illness can benefit greatly from these
physical effects.

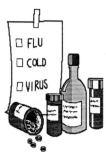

Many researchers have found that negative
emotions can influence the immune system.
Humor therapy allows POSITIVE emotions to
manipulate the immune system for POSITIVE
results. In contrast, the incidence of heart
attacks has been directly related to the
destructive emotions of fear and rage.

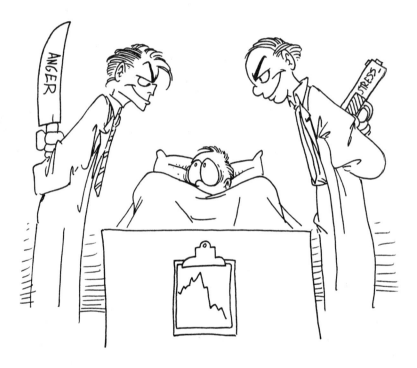

People who spend their time in resentment or in fear will have a greater chance of a heart attack. These two negative emotions can be assuaged and contravened by laughter. When we are afraid, we can laugh at the situation and alleviate our fear. Rage and anger can also be diminished by a healthy dose of humor. Thus, the use of humor can be a deterrent to heart attacks.

However laughter is regarded, there is general consensus that the results are physio-logically beneficial to human beings. Increased circulation and oxidation of the blood are good for all people, healthy or sick. The decrease of self-generated pain caused by tension is cer-tainly beneficial. In conclusion, we can all benefit from a good, deep, fully felt laugh.

3

Psychological Effects of Humor

A merry heart doeth good like medicine.
-- Proverbs 17:22

The power of humor to aid in conquering the pain and difficulties of life must be well known to comedians, cartoonists, and comedy writers. Recent research has shown that many people in these professions have previously experienced intense isolation, depression, suffering or loss.

Laughing at their personal traumas helped them to deal with their childhood difficulties. Their transition into careers related to humor was a natural way to continue the process of using humor to cope with stress and tension.

David Steinberg, Jackie Gleason, W. C. Fields, Dudley Moore, and Carol Burnett have all overcome early tragedy. For example, comedian Totie Field's mother died when Totie was five. Years later, Totie did a hilarious TV show even after she had become an amputee due to cancer. She kept her humor perspective and made others laugh while she battled a fatal illness.

These talented performers obviously agreed with George Bernard Shaw, who said:

> *We have no more right to consume happiness without producing it, than to consume wealth without producing it.*

Gail Sheehy's best-selling book, *Pathfinders*, described coping devices that "pathfinders" use to deal with life. The ability to see humor in a situation ranked high as a technique for overcoming life's crises. She reports that people who were filled with a sense of well-being survived the difficult passages of life by seeing humor in the situation. The ability to laugh in the face of a challenge is essential to mental health.

How can humor help us to cope with life's problems? There are four significant ways:

1. Laughter functions as a coping mechanism to relieve anxiety. It reduces stress and tension.

2. Humor is an outlet for hostility and anger. We can poke fun at the source of our irritation.

3. Humor provides an escape from reality and everyday cares. It allows us to forget our daily problems.

4. Laughter lightens the heavy emotions related to crisis, tragedy, chronic illness, disability, and death. Humor is a distancing mechanism when employed during tragic times. Laughter, as a coping

mechanism, has been used by successful
people throughout history.

Renowned for freeing the slaves, Abraham
Lincoln was also known to have used his sense
of humor to gain the strength and power to go on
during difficult times.

Many people are unaware of the setbacks
that Lincoln had before his successful election to
the Presidency of the United States. In earlier
times he had lost his job, failed in business, was
defeated in a bid for the state legislature, lost in
a bid for re-election to Congress, and twice was
defeated for the Senate. He also was beaten in an
effort to secure the nomination for Vice-
President. Soon after that, his sweetheart died.

In spite of all these setbacks and failure, he
summoned the courage to laugh at life and continue to seek his goals politically.

Setbacks and losses are a part of life. It is
how we view them that causes us much of our
mental anguish. Unfortunately, many people

derive a false picture of how life should be from movies and television. For those who grew up on weekly doses of "The Donna Reed Show" or "Leave it to Beaver," life seldom matches up with the rosy picture we saw. We saw people who never had to deal with death or illness, and then, we were unprepared to cope when we had to deal with either.

In present day television, young people are exposed to endless violence and are thus unprepared to deal with real-life violence, should it occur. This overexposure to violence can jade the view of life which they develop. Learning to accept and laugh at our difficulties when they arise will enable us to pick ourselves up and go on.

It is often not the major crises which do us in, but the little, everyday irritants which fester in our minds. In other words, we can frequently deal with the larger losses; but if someone cuts in front of us on the freeway, our anger seethes inside and hurts us. It is our reaction to the other driver which causes us unease.

We need instead to shift our perspective and focus on real life examples that make us laugh. Then, instead of being angry at other drivers, we can feel sorry for the stresses which cause them to drive recklessly.

Humor helps us shift perspective on our lives. It is a creative alternative to coping with stress.

Life is a tragedy when seen in close-up but a comedy in a long shot.

-- *Charlie Chaplin*

Is it a tragedy if someone cuts in front of us on the road? Is it a tragedy if we misplace a sock after doing the laundry? Is it a tragedy if we temporarily lose our car keys?

None of these are truly tragedies, and yet all of us have ruined perfectly nice days because they occurred. Laughing at ourselves and at our little difficulties can save us hours of anger and anguish.

An acquaintance recently celebrated his 91st birthday. When asked what he had to do to reach 100, his response was quick and succinct: "All I have to do is wait."

TWO

Making Humor

a Part of

Your Life

4

Humor and the Family

More marriages might survive if the partners realized that sometimes the better comes after the worse.

-- *Anonymous*

What do you think of when you walk down memory lane with your family? Do you recall many happy family gatherings filled with joy and harmony? Or do you, like most of us, recall some of the holiday disasters? No doubt about it; family life is not always all that its cracked up to be. For most of us family life is a mixed bag: sometimes happy, sometimes sad, sometimes downright unpleasant.

So if laughter is not the first sound that you remember when you think of your family, don't despair. We have all had to face the fact that our families were not as television used to portray them. Gone are the days when June Cleaver yelled "Dinner!" and Ward and the boys showed up instantly with their hands washed and heads filled with good humor.

Large families who sit down to break bread together went out with glass milk bottles and doctors who make house calls. Those of us who grew up with expectations of creating a family scene modeled after a Norman Rockwell cover for *Saturday Evening Post* have had to swallow a large dose of reality.

In the real world, family life is a mixture of love-hate relationships. So the picture you remember is probably more realistic than those who pretend that all was rosy and filled with glee. However, when we recall the good times, they are almost always associated with humor and fun.

Let's take a look at some family situations we all face and see how a sense of humor can ease the tension and let the good feelings flow.

Discipline

When and how to discipline children is one of the major challenges facing parents today. It can be a lot easier if we simply learn how to "lighten up." Lola shares a story where her ability to

think like a child enabled her to find a solution
to a "dirty" problem.

My husband, Hank, and I had to make some
drastic adjustments in our mental picture of
the perfect family to survive the childhood,
adolescence, and teenage years of our four
sons. Any success we may have had is attri-
butable to our efforts to see the humor in even
the most trying situations. The fact that the
four boys survived our efforts to discipline,
love, and form them can also be attributed to
the fact that they often provided the humor in
the situation just by being kids.

One of the most vivid examples of inserting a
lighter mood into a dark problem is one that
came to be known as "Mud Day." When our
two oldest sons were four and five years old,
we bought our first home in Houston, Texas. It
was brand new and we moved in before the
yard was planted. There was no grass in the
yard--just mud.

When the boys played in the yard, they got
mud all over their shoes, and when it dried, it
had to be pried off with a putty knife. We
called it "Texas Cement."

Obviously, I could have taken the easy way out
and just said "No" to playing in the sticky
stuff. But that would have been hard to enforce
and made the boys miserable. What to do?

I declared that one day a week would be cele-brated as "Mud Day." On that day, the boys were encouraged to play in the mud from sun-up to sundown. They had a ball, and they were the envy of the neighborhood kids. They squealed like two-legged pigs as they rolled around and threw mud balls at each other. Lunch was served outside on the picnic table. They hosed off their hands and faces before eating and did the same before the snack they had in the afternoon. Their happy laughter could be heard for miles around.

I seldom had to call them in at the end of the day. They were ready to get cleaned up on their own. They took off their clothes and I hosed them down. They squealed and laughed as the water hit its mark and revealed skin beneath all that Texas Cement.

The boys always ate their heartiest supper on Mud Day, and they were usually asleep before I even turned off the light in their bedroom. The rest of the week they genuinely tried to stay out of the Texas Cement. They were saving it up for Mud Day. What had been an ongoing aggravation was turned into a happy event through the use of humor and a sense of fun.

Raising children can be tiring and taxing. Perhaps, the next time you face a difficult situa-tion with your youngsters, you will remember Lola's Mud Day solution. Putting humor and fun into the problem will save the day for you and your children.

Holidays

Something that every home could use during the holidays is a bathroom scale that's seasonally adjusted.

-- Comedy Letter

Holidays can be stressful for every family member. It is a sad fact that more suicides occur during holiday seasons than at any other time. We all grow up with expectations of what each holiday should be like and how we will spend it with our families.

As we marry and our family grows, we begin to spend holidays with people who celebrate differently from the way we do, or do not celebrate at all. When this happens and we find that we must give up our childhood traditions, it can be very difficult for us.

The Gillebaards and the Lerners experienced slightly differing types of holiday pressures.

The Gillebaards had established a tradition of opening their Christmas gifts one present at a time and reading aloud the card that came with it. Many of the gifts were hidden somewhere around the house, and the first opening was only the beginning of a series of clues. One Christmas, it took the family eight hours to pursue each and every clue and to find all the gifts! After that year, they set a time limit.

When one of the boys was married, both families wanted the couple to spend Christmas with them. The newlyweds decided to spend one Christmas with her parents and next with his and alternate in the same way for Thanksgiving. The first Christmas was to be spent with the Gillebaards.

The new daughter-in-law quickly found out that things were going to be different when her husband disappeared several evenings, weeks before Christmas, in order to prepare all his clues. When Christmas came, she was ready for turkey and dressing long before it was

served. She could not believe the goings on
when the gift hunt began. She really missed
the kind of Christmas that she had grown up
with.

The next year, their son spent Christmas at his
in-laws' house. He told his parents later that
all the gifts were opened almost simul-
taneously, and that the whole celebration was
over before he knew it. He, too, missed his
family's kind of Christmas.

The Lerner's had a similar but slightly
different problem.

They had been married only a few months
when the dilemma of which parent to have
dinner with on which holiday became evident.
BOTH mothers wanted them present on
Mother's Day. On that first holiday after their
wedding they ate two complete dinners after
having driven more than an hour between the
two homes.

During the first year of their marriage, the pressures of trying to please both sets of parents intensified. Finally, after failing to reach a compromise with either set of parents, they found an alternative solution: They left town!

There is no easy solution to the stresses often created by family celebrations and holidays. The best we can offer is that you try to laugh at the problems instead of crying over them. Look for the humor in the situations your family usually gets upset about. Lower your expectations and take time to see the lighter side.

How can you look at the lighter side of a difficult family situation? Step back and view it from the perspective of a stranger. Remember, you are always more critical of your own flesh and blood. Hopefully, a new perspective will help you to see the lighter side of even the most stressful family difficulties.

Communication

Open communication is as important to a healthy family life as are laughter and fun. Lola's family developed a wonderful method to enhance its ability to communicate. They called it "Family Night."

Here's Lola's story:

I can honestly say that Family Night was one of the most precious parts of our lives. The actual rules, however, were very simple.

1. Every family member had to show up, no excuses. Any of us could bring a guest as long as a head count was turned in in time for me to put more water in the soup. (Having guests turned out to be an excellent idea; it often kept the family members from killing each other).

2. Each family member was required to share a humorous experience from the last week. (It's amazing what we found out about our kids through these stories.)

3. No interruptions of any kind from the outside world were permitted. This included TV, phone calls or later plans for the evening. (We always chose a night in the middle of the week).

4. No subject was ever taboo at these family nights and no judgements could be made on anything said at the table. Also, every personal thing discussed was to be considered confidential. (More on this later.)

When we first started our Family Night tradition, I had visions of my husband, Hank, and I filling the evening with one pithy quote after

another. There would be inspirational words that the kids would always remember and later pass on to their children.

No such luck! No matter where the conversation started, in our family the topic always ended up to be cars, sex, or money.

The valuable lesson that we learned, however, was that the topics really didn't matter. What was important was the humor and the honest, open communication that took place and the fun that we had doing it.

Family Night worked for us; why don't you give it a try?

Confidentiality

An issue closely related to communication is that of confidentiality. We cannot expect our family members to confide in us and share their personal situations when they know they are likely to be the subject of discussion with other family members and even friends.

When the authors compared notes from their own family experiences and later confirmed their findings with others, they found that nearly all families seemed to operate in one of two ways.

Some openly discuss everyone's business in-depth, while also adding their comments and criticisms. At the other extreme, families stay on safe ground, discussing the weather or local sports, while blissfully ignoring serious issues or problems and pretending that everything is just "wonderful."

Obviously, neither approach is desirable. We want to encourage open communication on any subject with the clear understanding that any family discussions are confidential. Gossip--which is hearing something you like about someone you don't--must be eliminated. Lola's family night would not have worked without their strong commitment to confidentiality.

This technique can even work with in-laws. Lola's daughter-in-law has told her that the biggest disappointment to her mom and dad is that she does not complain about Lola when she goes home.

Does this mean that Lola is the perfect mother-in-law? Not at all. It only means that Lola and her daughter-in-law have discussed, argued about, and laughed at their differences and aggravations over the years so that there is nothing left to gripe about. And, when and if there is, they direct it to each other during family night and thoroughly enjoy the session. AND, they do not gossip about it afterwards.

So, please take our advice. Make confidentiality the standard in your family communications. You will be amazed at the difference it will make.

Illness

Children somehow expect their parents to always be there, even when they have grown up and left home. The ways in which they handle unexpected illnesses is often bizarre, and sometimes very humorous. Lola shares an example from a holiday season four years ago:

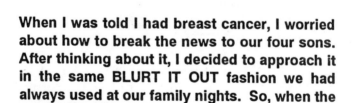

When I was told I had breast cancer, I worried about how to break the news to our four sons. After thinking about it, I decided to approach it in the same BLURT IT OUT fashion we had always used at our family nights. So, when the first one called on the phone:

"Hi, Mom."

"Hi, Babe."

"How are you?"

"Not too good, I'm afraid. I've just been told I have breast cancer.

(Long Pause) And then the kid says, "Does that mean you're going to die?"

The second one calls:

"Hi, Mom."

"Hi, Babe."

"What's up?"

"Nothing good, I'm afraid. I've just been told I have breast cancer.

(Long pause) "But, mom, you don't even eat fat."

The third one calls:

"Hi, Mom."

"Hi, Babe."

"How's life treating you?"

"Not well. I just found out I have breast cancer."

(Long pause) This isn't going to bother Dad, is it?"

The fourth one calls:

"Hi, Mom."

"Hi, Babe."

"What's new?"

"Nothing good. The doctor says I have cancer."

(Long pause) and then the kid says, "Why couldn't it have been Mrs. Fenley?"

All that took place on December 4, 1987. On Saturday, December 5, I went in for a chest X-ray and a bone scan. I had announced to the family that if the cancer had spread, I was not having the surgery. My husband wanted to go with me for the tests but I said, "No, I can only handle my own emotions at this time.

The tests took all day, but the doctors assured me that they saw no other cancerous tissue. I returned home exhausted, but excited about the good news. I still had lots of family nights to look forward to.

I jumped out of the car and started toward the front door. And then I heard the music bellowing loudly. It was Mahalia Jackson singing "Silent Night"!

I threw open the door and stepped inside the house. In the living room was the largest Christmas tree we have ever had. It was decorated with all the ornaments that every kid had made through the years, including the ugly ones.

Standing around the tree was my family, each one dressed in a suit and tie. They looked as if they were ready to carry me down the aisle in a box.

"Merry Christmas." they shouted.

"Merry Christmas," I whispered, "and a Happy New Year. I just found out that I have lots more to come."

I can honestly say that particular Family Night was the most precious that I have ever experienced. And I credit it all to my family's love of humor and fun, regardless of the circumstances.

One of the major stressors on any family is the serious, life-threatening illness of any of its members. If we can somehow find a way to bring a sense of fun and normalcy to the situation, it will make it a little easier to get through these very bad times.

> *You grow up the day you have the first real laugh, at yourself.*
>
> *-- Ethel Barrymore*

5

Humor on the Job

Take time to work -- It is the price of success.
Take time to think -- It is the source of power.
Take time to laugh -- It is the music of the
soul.

-- *"Old English Prayer"*

Today's workplace, unfortunately, is seldom a place that either the employer or the employee goes to have fun. TGIF--Thank God It's Friday--has become a commonplace expression celebrating the fact that the workweek is finally coming to an end.

In view of what is going on in many companies today, these feelings are not all that surprising. Conflicts are a common occurrence. Harassment cases make the headlines on a regular basis. Bosses blame their employees and the employees blame the company. The number of Worker's Compensation stress claims is increasing geometrically each year.

Many people keep their jobs only for the money:

Money is better than poverty, if only for financial reasons.

-- *Woody Allen*

Given this workaday environment, what can we do to make our jobs more enjoyable and less stressful? One answer is to make our jobs more fun by injecting a little humor into our day-to-day activities.

Humor has many on-the-job advantages. When used appropriately, it can:

1. Manage conflict

Difficult people never die--they just reproduce faster! We are not going to be able to rid ourselves of them, so we must do the next best thing: learn how to deal with them.

We can begin doing this by realizing that the only person you can truly manage is yourself. By learning to use humor in conflict situations, we will be better able to cope. One often-quoted example is to picture angry or disagreeable co-workers standing in front of us in their underwear. By creating an absurd picture in our minds, we reduce the tension and fear and we are better able to deal with any situation.

2. Motivate others

Happy employees are productive employees. We believe that every employee can contribute to overall morale by introducing some humor into the day-to-day work environment. Most workers could use a "humor fix." If we can't provide one for ourselves, then we can look for a funny friend.

3. Relieve stress

Stewart experienced a real-life illustration of how innovative employees dealt with a highly stressful work environment by using humor.

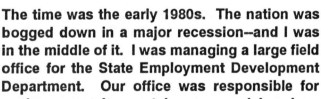

The time was the early 1980s. The nation was bogged down in a major recession--and I was in the middle of it. I was managing a large field office for the State Employment Development Department. Our office was responsible for paying unemployment insurance claims in a county where the unemployment rate had increased ten-fold.

Working conditions were extremely stressful. Regardless of the temperatures or weather conditions, there were more than 100 people waiting for the doors to open at 8:00 a.m.

every morning. The doors would have to be monitored and people turned away beginning at 4:30 p.m. each day so that we could take care of the people already in the building by our 5:00 closing time.

Lines were very long, with waits in excess of one hour common. We simply did not have enough staff to handle the exploding workload.

The employees we did have were wonderful. They came early and stayed late; they worked through their breaks and into their lunch hours. The public seemed to sense that the employees were doing their best for them. Despite the long waits and crowded conditions, we seldom had any incidents arise.

However, after days and weeks of this type of pressure, staff morale was growing thin. Then, Halloween arrived.

Several of the staff members came to me and asked if the staff could dress in costumes for Halloween. I was concerned about the reaction of a large number of unemployed people to an apparent party going on while they were waiting for service. Yet, I also felt that, if handled correctly, a Halloween celebration might help our sagging morale. So I asked our people to see if they could come up with a way that the public could be made a part of our activities--and they responded!

The office was decorated festively. Candy and popcorn were available throughout the office, and I wish you could have seen the costumes! Staff members were dressed as witches, goblins, bumblebees, and birds. There was even a pregnant ballerina.

Just before the doors opened, the people waiting outside were treated to a Disneyland-like parade of characters. Our costumed staff shook hands and welcomed the people as they entered the office. Then work went on as usual. Throughout the day, however, both our employees and the public enjoyed the costumes and camaraderie that resulted. There were two incidents in particular that I always remember with a smile.

I was walking through the office and noticed a gentleman sitting alone, apparently waiting for service. I asked him if he had been helped. He grinned and said, "Yes, the old witch is bringing me my check."

Later, I passed a desk where another gentleman was, unfortunately, being denied benefits
because he had quit his job. He was laughing
uncontrollably. As he was told by the "pregnant ballerina" that he would not be eligible for
benefits, he got up, still laughing and said, "Its
OK, lady, it was worth it."

The day was a roaring success, with both the
employees and the public enjoying it
thoroughly. For weeks afterward, photographs
that had been taken were looked at, discussed,
and enjoyed over and over again. Morale in
the office remained high, as the staff was able
to use the memories, the laughter, and good
fellowship that was shared on this one day to
get them through the many long and stressful
days that were to follow. The humor also
resulted in a "bonding" among our employees
that I do not believe could have taken place in
any other way.

4. Lighten the load

Let's look at one more of Stewart's real-life
experiences.

Coincidentally, I also saw humor used to raise
morale on another Halloween; this one much
more recent. A small company for which I
consult had just gone through their first layoff
and were very upset and worried about it. In

**the executive offices, some of the manage-
ment staff decided to cheer up the president.**

**While the president was out for a meeting, they
decorated his office, complete with spider
webs, bats, and broomsticks. On his desk
they placed a large crystal ball. When the
president arrived, one of the employees,
dressed as a fortune teller, proceeded to tell
his fortune and predict the company's outstanding success over the upcoming year.
This was done in a very humorous manner and
raised the spirits of all concerned. And, by the
way, the prediction came true! The company
was able to reverse its negative trend and
experience good financial success during the
next year—despite the recession.**

The above are just a few examples of how
humor can be used to defuse stresses and negative situations in the workplace. It is inexpensive
and easy to swallow medicine for whatever ails
us--or our companies.

Remember, also, that the worksite, by its
very nature, produces some level of stress. But,
as we all know, there is good stress and there is
bad stress. We need to alleviate the bad stress by
learning to see the humor in even the most negative situations. This is a skill we can all learn.

The "Old English Prayer" with which we began this chapter expresses it very well and is worth repeating.

> *Take time to work -- It is the price of success.*
> *Take time to think -- It is the source of power.*
> *Take time to laugh -- It is the music of the soul.*

Pitfalls of Inappropriate Humor

While humor used properly can reap significant benefits, humor used in inappropriate ways can cause serious problems, particularly in a business setting.

What is inappropriate humor? If even ONE person is offended by it, the humor may be inappropriate. If we accept this definition, it means that we must carefully analyze the audience and the situation to ensure that both our words and our message are appropriate.

What are some specific examples of inappropriate humor in the workplace?

1. Humor that "puts down" the company. This is both disloyal and dangerous to employee morale.

2. Humor that "puts down" other employees. This creates distance and disharmony and discourages bonding. This type of negative humor should be directed only at YOURSELF.

3. Racist/ethnic humor. We never know who may be insulted or whether our attempts at humor could be considered harassment.

4. Sexual or sexist humor. A good example is the "Dumb Blonde" jokes which made the rounds of many companies recently. While some women enjoyed these jokes, many others were offended.

We can generally tell if our humor is inappropriate by the manner in which people react to it. Dead giveaways are silence, nervous laughter, pulling away, or even tears.

Remember, in addition to hurting feelings, sexual and other forms of harassment directed against any group protected by Title VII of the Civil Rights Act can form the basis for legal action against the company or individuals. Most companies will take a dim view of this type of humor, no matter how innocent the intent. Here, we are better off safe rather than sorry.

Humor in Management

Successful administrators and managers use humor as an integral part of their management style. They realize that the key to effective management always lies in successful human relations. We also know that wherever two or more employees work together on a long-term basis, conflict is inevitable.

The larger our work force, the higher the incidence of conflict. Defusing the anger through humor can help us to resolve that conflict. It's hard for two people to stay angry when they are laughing together. Laughter is a harmonious act which stimulates a positive, rather than a negative emotional climate.

The challenge is that negative emotions are a bugaboo to open communication. It's hard to be open and warm when we are fostering resentments or fears. The good news is that humor can change this negative climate.

SuZette Alger, a corporate productivity specialist, shared the following story with us.

In a manufacturing company with which I consult, the General Manager was always reminding the Engineering Manager of a mistake his department had made. The poor fellow was sorry, and had made corrections so the mistake would not happen again. Yet, his boss continually reminded him of his past error.

Finally, I took the manager aside and said: "The next time he says that, agree with him and then just ask: 'By the way, when does the statute of limitations run out on this mistake?'"

Everyone laughed, and they now use that line around the company constantly. It means, "OK, we made a mistake. Now let's forget it and get on with our success."

Tension and stress cost companies a great deal of money in lack of productivity and absenteeism. Employers who use humor in their management style and encourage their employees to see the light side of situations are, in fact, improving the profit margin of their business.

Remember how the song, "Whistle While You Work," from the Disney classic "Snow White," encouraged the dwarfs to find pleasure in their efforts? Employees who find pleasure in their workplace will also be more productive.

Recent studies have shown that humor has a definite bonding effect upon groups and builds an attitude of teamwork. When employees laugh together and build a warm, cohesive group spirit, they produce more.

Despite the feelings between workers, however, the management style of a company will dictate the amount of humor in the workplace. Managers who believe that using humor with their employees diminishes their authority are losing a valuable opportunity to improve personal relations with their employees.

This kind of heavy-handed, authoritarian style of management fosters absenteeism and builds resentment in the employees. Remember, if they're not laughing with us, they may be laughing at us.

Some managers believe that laughter is inappropriate at work. These people support the Puritan work ethic which demands that work should not be pleasurable. They fail to understand that when laughter and pleasure are injected into the work place, employees are more eager to be there and to perform their tasks efficiently.

Certainly it is inappropriate for employees and managers to be guffawing and cutting up in front of waiting customers. However, as in the Halloween example discussed earlier, we find that customers, too, like the use of appropriate humor in the workplace.

We are not advocating that we wear funny hats and fake noses to work every day and tell shaggy dog jokes. Managers and business leaders are not comedians. Neither should we allow employees to waste valuable work time joking around or on other forms of levity. As business leaders, we must control what is the appropriate environment for the workplace and ensure that a proper balance is maintained.

Even given the above, however, the development of a positive influence on our employees needs to be a primary goal of our management style. We don't want to beat the point to death, but happy employees are productive employees.

We begin to enhance our management style by carefully considering the type of humor that is right for us. We must determine both the appropriateness and the style of humor that we will use. It is important that we never use a form of humor which demeans us or our employees nor one that devalues the work problems which we face.

Some managers are low key users of wit and satire. Others favor puns and playing on words. Several forms of humor can be effectively used by anyone, regardless of management style or personality.

The first of these is humorous quotes. George Bernard Shaw said, "I often quote myself. It adds spice to my conversation." Quotes are appropriate in memos and in speeches.

If you are faced with a speaking situation which has a really deadly topic, humorous quotes can help to keep your audience awake. Mark Twain and Winston Churchill are excellent sources for these.

Cartoons provide an excellent source of material for speakers in business. Describing a cartoon is an effective way to insert humor. Even more effective is to show the cartoon on an overhead projector. There is a built-in insurance policy in the use of a cartoon. If someone doesn't find it funny, you didn't create it.

Training of employees provides a great opportunity to set the tone with humor. Research has revealed that adults learn best in a pleasant, relaxed atmosphere. If we are teaching new, more productive techniques of how to accomplish a job, we can often get our employees to laugh at the old, less productive methods. We can exaggerate them to bring out the humor.

Another way to insert humor is to point out humorous examples of our personal trials when trying to learn new techniques or strategies. Once they see that we are not too serious and uptight, they will relate better to us and learn even more.

In Section 3 of this book, we will show you how to develop more humor strategies that you can use to enhance your working environment. Give them a try. They may assist you in obtaining recognition and even advancement. At the very least, they will make your job a lot more fun.

6

Humor, Health, and Lifestyle

The man who makes everything that leads to happiness depend upon himself, and not other men, has adopted the very best plan for living happily.

-- *Plato*

In today's high-tech society, we are bombarded with so much information that it is impossible to assimilate it all. In many professions, such as the medical field, it is literally impossible for a professional to keep up with all the new technology and research.

This "information boom" does, however, allow us to be better informed and to take action rather than be merely passive observers. When we can include humor in the participation process, both our health and our overall well-being will be enhanced.

Experts differ in their advice and suggestions for what constitutes a healthy lifestyle. One expert may advise you to take all dairy products out of your diet, while another will advise you to drink more milk.

We believe that it is important for you to get to know yourself and to determine the best course of action for your life, based on your uniqueness. Our goal in this discussion is to increase your awareness and to enhance your knowledge so that you can make better informed choices to improve the quality of your life.

It is essential that we evaluate our values, goals, and lifestyle on a regular basis in order to maintain the quality of life we are seeking. We must continually review to determine what is and what is not working for us. In this chapter, we will offer suggestions on how to reduce stress and live a happy, healthy lifestyle while also developing a healthy sense of humor.

We must cultivate our garden.
                                        -- Voltaire

One way to begin is by clarifying and under-standing your values.

If your lifestyle is in conflict with your guid-ing principles, you cannot help but experience stress on an ongoing basis. What are **your** values?

Do you have a personalized license plate or a bumper sticker on your car? If so, does it reflect your philosophy or lifestyle? If not, what would you like it to say?

As we indicated earlier, if your day-to-day actions or activities are in conflict with your governing values, you cannot help but experi-ence stress.

Lorrie was working with a gentleman who indicated that one of his highest values was his family. When asked how much time he spent with his family each week, he replied, "I don't spend much time with them; I'm too busy." After further questioning, she determined that he spent only 30 to 40 minutes at dinner time with his wife and four children.

This obvious incongruence between his values and his actions was causing him consid-erable unhappiness and stress. As a beginning step, Lorrie helped him to work out an imple-mentation strategy which took only two minutes per family member to accomplish.

His two-minute process included walking around the block with his wife as soon as he came home from work, telling a short story to each of his two youngest children, going outside and playing catch for a couple of minutes with one teen-age son, and then with his more expressive son, sitting down to look at drawings or listen to stories or poetry. During these two minutes per person, he agreed not to criticize or judge. Instead, he listened and gave positive, supportive feedback to each person.

In addition, at dinner time, each family member shared at least one great thing that happened to him/her that day. Often, the stories were humorous and the whole family was able to laugh together.

In a very short period of time, his relation-ship with his family improved and the family dinner became a pleasant, positive time for interaction. From that humble two-minute beginning, the man was able to reshape his family life into the important role he had always wanted it to have.

Life is like that, something like walking a tightrope. Imagine walking along, feeling invigo-rated and on target. Life is great! Then all of a sudden, a gust of wind blows and you almost fall off the tightrope. Now your heart is beating fast, you feel tense, and yes, you are scared. At this point, you have two choices. You either stop and climb down to a safe place, or you continue on your life's journey despite your trepidation.

There is a fine line between balance and imbalance. What works for one person may not work at all for the next. To reach our most productive and healthy levels, we need a balanced lifestyle, which incorporates the physical, mental, emotional, and spiritual parts of our nature. And if we can throw in sprinklings of humor along the way, all the better.

The **H** in humor is for "**h**ealth." It could also be for "**h**appy" because happy people tend to be healthier people. There are four natural tranquilizers: laughter, music, exercise, and sex.

Each of these causes the body to release endorphins, a pain-killing chemical that truly can ease a backache or relax a headache. However, of the four tranquilizers, laughter is the only one that we always can carry with us and which requires no special equipment, not even the agreement of two consenting adults!

With that thought in mind, let's now look at each of the four major areas of a balanced lifestyle and see if we can apply the lessons we have learned.

Physical

To create humor and a sense of playfulness during physical activity, it helps if you participate with the type of people who make you laugh and feel good. This is why people prefer the social atmosphere of fitness centers to exercising alone. Even those who do not talk to others will often listen to music or other tapes on earphones while walking on the treadmill or climbing the Stairmaster. Have you ever watched weight lifters working as a team and encouraging each other on to greater and greater accomplishments?

There are, of course, many alternatives to fitness centers or gyms.

Lorrie shares her experience with dancing:

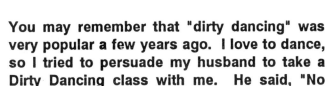

You may remember that "dirty dancing" was very popular a few years ago. I love to dance, so I tried to persuade my husband to take a Dirty Dancing class with me. He said, "No way. You take it and then you can teach me."

Although I was a little nervous, particularly about dancing too closely with strangers, I decided to take the class without him. I pictured the instructor as a handsome hunk, like Patrick Swayze. Instead, a balding, middle-aged man with thick-rimmed glasses and flood-length polyester pants entered the room and began to take roll. While we were all still waiting for our instructor, the man began to teach the class.

What a surprise! He turned out to be a fantastic teacher, even if he didn't look anything like Patrick. He even taught us how to dirty dance and still keep a distance from our partner if we wanted to.

As Lorrie found out, there are many ways to exercise and have fun at the same time. But even without exercise, a little mirth can do a lot for a person's physical health. Dr. William Fry of Stanford University Medical School calls laughter "internal jogging" and cites evidence that it exerts a beneficial effect on most of the body's major physical systems. He found that intense laughter can actually double the heart rate for three to five minutes. That's good news for many of us, since it is a great deal easier to laugh during the day than it is to do aerobics.

Emotional

We can enhance our emotional well-being by understanding one simple fact: Laughter makes us feel good, and it's hard to feel bad when you're feeling good. People who have discovered the humor habit--the habit of making life fun and seeing the humor in everyday situations--will have far fewer emotional crises with which to deal.

One of these situations was brought home to Lola recently when her husband, Hank, decided to give up smoking cigarettes.

Hank is a man who never left home without a full pack of cigarettes in his pocket. He lit up before every phone call. He never made a business decision without first taking a drag from that cigarette. He blew smoke rings as he

propped his feet up on his desk and visualized his next entrepreneurial idea.

However, Hank's family had a history of lung cancer, and the doctor told him that he would be a part of that history if he didn't stop smoking. This threat was underlined when Hank saw the X-rays of his tar-filled lungs. He threw a half pack of cigarettes into the garbage can as he left the doctor's office. He also stopped at the pharmacy and brought a big rubber pacifier which he hung around his neck.

He sucked on that pacifier a lot during the next few weeks. Did it cure his craving for cigarettes? Of course not. But it did give him something to do when the craving hit. That pacifier also got the attention of everyone with whom he came in contact. Hank explained that he was giving up smoking and people understood. People also smiled--and laughed; and Hank laughed with them. After all, there is something ridiculous about a grown man with a full beard sucking on a pacifier. The point is that the pacifier--and the laughter--gave Hank the emotional support he needed to beat one of the toughest addictions.

Emotional well-being often includes having some type of support system. We need to understand that this support will not always come from those we love. We sometimes need to seek the support we need through peer groups or special interest groups. Organizations such as

Alcoholics Anonymous learned the power of peer support many years ago. We all need to spend time with positive, happy, and supportive people.

Mental

Imagine that your mind is a sponge, always ready to absorb new information. When you do not nourish it, it dries up, shrinks, and eventually begins to deteriorate. Instead, you can learn to stimulate your mind and enjoy learning new things.

The authors recently read a story about a woman in her eighties who had just graduated from college. When she was just beginning, many of her well-meaning friends told her that she was crazy to go to school at her age. It would take her at least four years to finish and she would be 86 years old. She responded that in four years she would be 86 with or without the degree, and she would rather have the degree! We all need to remember this story when we think it's too late for us to learn or to accomplish a goal.

Before you go to bed at night, take a few minutes to read about an inspirational person-- someone whom you would like to emulate.

In addition, you can regularly feed your mind some humorous material. Read joke books or anecdotes about famous people. We strongly recommend George Burns, one of our favorites, who has written a number of warm and humorous autobiographical books.

This type of positive mental stimulation will give you the strength and mental attitude that you will need to deal with the many nay-sayers with whom you will come in contact during the next 24 hours.

Spiritual

One's spiritual life, of course, is highly personal. Each of us needs to develop our own sense of spiritual well-being. Yours may include organized religion, prayer, meditation, contemplation, or simply communing with nature. Lorrie recalls an incident at church:

The minister, a tall, thin, rather formal man was preaching the Sunday sermon, a lesson in Christian morality.

In the midst of his rather bland delivery, he began to hear the pulsating beat of rap music, which gradually became louder and louder. All of the parishioners could hear the blasting rhythm as a car stopped in front of the church. The minister stopped momentarily and did a double take.

Then, with his hands remaining firmly on the pulpit, the minister resumed his sermon. However, his body, almost involuntarily,

responded to the call of the driving beat. First his shoulders and then his whole torso began to sway to the rhythm. Then his words began to bounce to the rhythm of the beat.

The congregation tried to stifle their laughter at the incongruity between the message and the messenger. This became known as our church's first rap sermon.

We believe that spiritual well-being also includes laughter and joy, unconditional love, and a sense of thankfulness and gratitude. Psalm 118:24 says it very well:

This is the day the Lord has made;
let us rejoice and be glad in it."

7

Using Humor to Deal with Grief and Loss

A joy shared is doubled; a grief shared is halved.

Anonymous

Each of us already has or will have to face the death of a loved one. Grieving can be a long and painful process and, for some, almost over-whelming. Humor can help us to restore a semblance of normalcy during a time when all seems lost. To illustrate this point, Lorrie will share with you her own personal experience and how she was able to use humor as a coping mechanism.

Lorrie's Story

My husband, Chris, and I often discussed whether we wanted to have children. We both wanted different things at different times. At one point, Chris was ready to be a parent, and I wasn't; then I was ready, and he wasn't. We ping-ponged back and forth for months. Then we agreed: Let's have a baby!

Six weeks later, we discovered that I had become pregnant on Labor Day. The pregnancy was normal: lots of morning sickness, water retention, irritability, and Big Mac attacks. We became best friends with a couple whom we met in childbirth class. We ate dinner with them, talked about parenthood, and played cards and games together once or twice a week.

The birth was difficult and long. There were some problems which forced an emergency Cesarean section. Our little boy was immediately put on life support.

A few days after our son was born, our friends from childbirth class had a healthy baby boy. Over the next couple of weeks, our relationship with them became strained, and we saw them only a few more times. They quit inviting us over and stopped returning our phone calls. Chris and I were both really hurt and confused. Since then, we've learned that, in our society, when people feel uncomfortable in the face of adversity, they often turn away.

In less than one week after birth, the respirator had been removed and Jared was breathing on his own. Then the doctors gave us the bad news: Because of the oxygen deprivation suffered during birth, Jared had severe brain damage. He couldn't suck, cry, or swallow. He was blind and deaf. With much patience, the nurses taught us how to care for our son and, after seven weeks in intensive care, Jared came home.

Once Jared was at home, nurses and other medical professionals helped us to give him the continuous care and attention that he needed. Jared was in and out of the hospital numerous times. The surgeries, treatments, medications, and other procedures which he had to endure was hard on us and harder on him. Jared's struggle ended Thursday, April 17, 1986 at 10:35 p.m.

How I Coped With My Loss

Instead of dwelling on the many challenges and difficult times we faced with Jared, we focused on all the wonderful things which we had been able to do together.

I recalled the times at 3:00 in the morning when I'd slip into the Neonatal Intensive Care Unit and see the nurses holding the tiny babies, swaying to the dance music playing on the radio. I'd smile and laugh, then hurry back to Jared and hold him close to me.

I felt better when I remembered the day my best friend and her children were visiting from Sam Diego. We were dressing Jared to go out, and we decided to spike his hair! We jelled it, and it stuck straight up! During the process, my friend's daughter took the shoes off her doll and put them on Jared. They fit perfectly. They were a light brown, slip-on oxford. What a cool kid! He really looked jazzy, and gave us all a good laugh. Then we all strolled together aboard the Queen Mary.

I recall the times that Jared attended exercise classes that I taught. All the participants were so loving and understanding. I still get a warm feeling when I remember the love, compassion, and support I received from my students. They made a difference in my life.

I can't overemphasize how much friends and family helped. Chris and I found that when we could talk, laugh, and cry with others, we began to heal our own broken hearts.

The other thing that helped me through the grief process was my ability to somehow find humor and joy, and to laugh. I found that every time I laughed, I felt better. So I began seeking out things that would bring me pleasure. Since I had enjoyed "I Love Lucy" so much as a child, I started watching the show again--sometimes once or twice a day. It would make me laugh, and I would feel better.

Another positive step was to join a peer support group called HOPING, which is an acronym for "Helping Other Parents In Normal Grieving." Chris and I learned how to use writing, drawing, and other expressive techniques to help us to express our grief and love for Jared.

Jared died just a month and a half before he would have been one year old. On his birthday, our entire family went to the bluffs in Long Beach with a balloon bouquet. The balloons read "Happy First Birthday." We each wrote our own messages on the balloons with markers before we released them to the heavens.

We looked out to the ocean, and we could feel the sea breezes blowing in our faces. As we sang "Happy Birthday" to Jared, we released all the balloons. To our delight and wonder, the balloons floated up and out to sea--the very sea where we had scattered Jared's ashes.

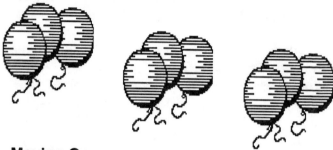

Moving On with My Life

A couple of months after Jared's death, I began work at a psychiatric and chemical dependency hospital as a Recreational Therapist. (Recreational therapy is an adjunctive therapy designed to create a healthy lifestyle physically, emotionally, mentally, and spiritually through leisure.)

Many of the patients were dealing with unresolved grief. I helped them to express their feelings and to begin the healing process. I found that my personal healing process continued as I helped them to heal.

In looking back, what helped Chris and me in our grieving was: (1) learning about the grief process itself, (2) having a support system (friends and family), (3) expressing our feelings by talking, writing, and drawing, (4) creating rituals (e.g., sending Jared a balloon on his birthday), and (5) learning to laugh and play again.

I was later introduced to guided imagery and clinical hypnotherapy. I discovered that I could learn about myself, relax, and feel a sense of peace and pleasure during guided imagery sessions.

In summary, our grieving has been a process. It is like a river, and sometimes we get caught up in an eddy, swirling around and around. When this happens, we need the support of others. They help us and we help them. Sometimes we let the current take us down the river of life; at other times, we fight it the entire way.

When we fight the pains of grief, we become exhausted and depleted. However, when we flow with it, we can begin to relax and see the beauty of the shores and the other miracles around us.

After my son's death, I decided to focus my studies on humor and grief. I began my research and in 1990 completed my thesis, *A Program Manual Incorporating Humor as a Therapeutic Adjunct in Bereavement Support Groups.* The dedication reads:

> *This work is dedicated to my beloved son, Jared Braden Boyd, who in his short life changed mine.*

Humor and the Grief Process

The grief process is the normal response to loss, and it can affect our entire life: physically, emotionally, mentally, and spiritually. During the grief process, we feel an overwhelming mixture of emotions, including anger, sadness, fear, hopelessness, and hurt.

States of grief include: first, shock and denial; second, anger and depression; and third, understanding and acceptance. There are also mini cycles within the larger cycle of the grief process. Such events as anniversary dates, birthdays, holidays, and dates of death can send grievers into mini grief cycles. The duration and intensity of these stages will vary, depending on the type of loss, how long it has been, and the cause of the loss.

The grief experience also changes over time. The intensity will tend to lessen unless there is "unresolved grief." Unresolved grief occurs when we suppress our feelings and do not allow ourselves to express the pain.

We are healed out of a suffering only by experiencing it to the full.

-- Marcel Proust

Along with understanding and acceptance, we need also to begin to reintroduce humor and joy into our lives. Many experts believe that humor is absolutely necessary for survival, longevity, and mental health. As discussed earlier in this book, it not only can heal physical illness but it can fill a variety of psychological, social, and emotional needs. It protects us from our fears and allows us to escape from an all-too-rational world.

One of the most popular TV shows of all time---M*A*S*H---gave us a clear demonstration of how doctors and nurses were able to escape the grief and horrors of war by somehow finding humor even as they dealt with the wounded and dying.

Dr. Bernie Siegel relates his views on laughter and the grief process in his book, *Love, Medicine, and Miracles*.

Frequently when I'm in a hospital room with a "dying" patient, we are laughing. Out in the hallway the other staff members often think we are denying reality. We must realize that people aren't "living" or "dying," they are either alive or dead. As long as they are alive, we must treat them this way. For this reason, I find the word 'terminal' very upsetting. It means we've begun to treat that person as though he or she were already dead, incapable of laughter and joy.

Perhaps the best way to end this chapter is to share a sign that was posted on a hospital bulletin board. It read:

Research shows that the first five minutes of life can be the most risky.

A hospital humorist had added:

The last five minutes ain't so hot, either!

THREE

Sharpening Your

Humor Funnybone

8

Measuring Your Humor Quotient

Humor could be falling downstairs, if you do
it in the act of warning your wife not to.
Kenneth Bird

The purpose of this chapter is to discuss your very own humor quotient, using the following ten questions as a guideline. This chapter will NOT discuss whether or not you have a sense of humor, for the authors believe that everyone does. Individual humor tastes do vary, but everyone has a laughing place (discussed in **Chapter 9, How to Find Humor**).

This is not a test, so you do not have to answer these questions. However, if you choose to, please respond honestly. You'll find that the questions are really easy. Just circle a number between 1 and 10 that best reflects your answer to each question.

In order to get the greatest benefit out of this "test," however, there are some additional "rules" you MUST follow. Do not begin until you have completely memorized the rules.

1. Use a #2 pencil. If you are right-handed, put the pencil in your <u>left</u> hand and vice versa.

2. If you are standing up, sit down. If you are sitting down, stand up.

3. Do not smile or show signs of enjoyment at any time during the test. This will invalidate your score and could result in a mandatory retest. (Additional forms are available at grossly inflated prices.)

The Test

1. How often do you release a genuine belly laugh to the point of side pains?

Seldom   Often

1   2   3   4   5   6   7   8   9   10

2. Do you find it easy to laugh any time, any place?

No   Yes

1   2   3   4   5   6   7   8   9   10

3. How often do you laugh when you are experiencing stress in your daily activities?

Seldom   Often

1   2   3   4   5   6   7   8   9   10

4. Do you think people who laugh at work are
    not working?

    Yes   No

    1   2   3   4   5   6   7   8   9   10

5. If you won the lottery, would you keep your
    job?

    Not a chance   Yes

    1   2   3   4   5   6   7   8   9   10

6. Is it possible to enjoy your job even if your
    boss is a jerk?

    Not probable   But possible

    1   2   3   4   5   6   7   8   9   10

7. Do you feel you laugh more when you have
    had a few drinks?

    Yes   No

    1   2   3   4   5   6   7   8   9   10

8. Do you ever laugh at yourself?

    No   Yes

    1   2   3   4   5   6   7   8   9   10

9. When embarrassed, do you laugh or get angry?

Angry   Laugh

1   2   3   4   5   6   7   8   9   10

10. Do you enjoy watching children at play?

Heck, no!   Yes

1   2   3   4   5   6   7   8   9   10

Now that you've finished, you can determine your score by simply totaling all the numbers that you circled.

A score of 70 or more is a signal that your humor potential is above average and that minimum adjustments are necessary. In fact, you could probably get a job teaching traffic school! If your score exceeds 80, please contact the authors. We need help in creating the next test!

If your score is between 40 and 70, you need a little more levity in your life. Find a funny friend.

If your score is below 40, you need a major humor tune-up. Spend an evening at the Improv with your funny friend.

Now, let's take a look at each of the questions individually.

1. How often do you release a genuine belly laugh to the point of side pains?

Many people cannot remember when they last had a side-aching belly laugh. This type of laughter is rare. It's not the kind of jolly belly wiggle we associate with good ole Santa Claus. A side-aching belly laugh can cripple the strongest man and bring the most dignified woman to the point of collapse. An expression like "I was laughing so hard I fell on the floor with tears in my eyes" is a good example of a side-aching belly laugh.

This type of laughter produces lots of endorphins, a chemical in the body that acts as a natural tranquilizer. After every side-aching belly laugh comes a period of total relaxation and contentment.

2. Do you find it easy to laugh any time, any place?

Humor is like luck. There's no telling when the mistress of opportunity might knock. If we do not take advantage of her generosity when she presents it, we may miss out. Humor is very similar. For no apparent reason, we may feel the urge to laugh.

Our body needs laughter as much as it needs tears, breathing, and eating. Suppressing humor is unhealthy, and it can actually prevent us from laughing. When our natural humor is not allowed to release itself, that positive energy becomes negative energy and emerges as tension, bitterness, and anger. Besides, it's been said that suppressed laughter goes down and makes our hips spread!

However, it's true that not all times are appropriate for laughter. We have to gauge our surroundings. If we want to laugh, but not in front of present company, we should excuse ourselves and then go laugh. We should not worry about embarrassing ourselves. People stare only because they want in on the joke. Everyone likes to laugh, and the whole world wants to go out to play.

3. How often do you laugh when you are experiencing stress in your daily activities?

Work is generally the highest cause of stress. However, many people rate interacting with their family and friends as equally stressful. To these people, family and friends ARE work! Anyone who has ever stayed with a hyperactive child can appreciate the feeling of dread which some parents get on the way home.

There are also friends whom we consider "work." You know the kind . . . the ones who make us want to jump behind the sofa and hide when we see their car in the driveway. We find ourselves making excuses not to see them. Beware! These friends can be expensive--not financially, but emotionally.

Most people agree that leisure is the least stressful activity in which we engage. By definition, leisure is directly opposite to work. When we think of work, we associate words like stress-filled, underpaid, and overworked. Leisure conjures up peaceful moments, relaxing times, and a feeling of utter contentment. However, vacations can sometimes be stressful! Ever take your visiting relatives to Disneyland?

The importance of knowing our stress levels at leisure as contrasted with work is to identify those elements that indeed do make leisure so stress-free. For one thing, leisure time makes fewer demands on us, and we have fewer responsibilities. Therefore, we are more relaxed.

It is important to remember that stress is not always a bad thing. It can be a great motivator. The pressure of stress gets us moving and gets things done. That's why we equate stress with work.

4. Do you think people who laugh at work are not working?

Modern medicine has proven that humor is therapeutic. As well as being good medicine, humor is a wonderful motivator, stimulator, and mood elevator. Workplaces that incorporate humor are introducing those elements that we find when we are at leisure. We are relaxed to the point of comfortableness, just enough to laugh more. Laughter helps to reduce tension and stress. It clears the mind so that the employee can become more focused on the project at hand. Thus, employees become more productive.

An employee looks forward to going to work because he or she feels productive, active, and needed. An atmosphere that is conducive to humor is a much more pleasant environment in which to work than one of fear. Also, because employees enjoy the atmosphere at work, there is less absenteeism and tardiness.

Humor is a great source of stimulation. It can increase a person's memory by 250%. That means that if we have an employee with no memory quotient at all, we can improve that memory significantly just by adding humor.

Humor grabs people's attention and keeps them interested. To prove this, try talking with a child. When the conversation becomes dull, the child's eyes go into "park." Let that child know that there is laughter available, and you have an energetic listener.

Humor elevates people. Everyone has a down day now and then. Laughter makes us feel better and helps us to realize that things are not so bad. Besides, humor is less expensive than shopping and spending money--and far more effective!

There are times when we get so bogged down with work that we become overwhelmed and begin to lose our concentration. Our mind flashes on many different things at once, affording none of them quality thought. Humor gives the mind and the body a break. It clears the mind of clutter and stimulates a more focused and productive atmosphere.

5. If you won the lottery, would you keep your job?

Although it's true that money can motivate an employee, it is not the sole determinant of what makes a happy employee. Those who enjoy what they are doing are the ones who become truly successful. They receive the raises, the promotions, and the attention of the employer.

Money is a fringe benefit. It is the enjoyment of the task that motivates the successful few. If we can find the activities that we love to do, the money will follow.

Always ask yourself, "Would I do this job for free?" If the answer is "no," then the job is only temporary. Sooner or later, you'll tire of it and either quit or get fired.

6. Is it possible to enjoy your job, even if your boss is a jerk?

All bosses can be jerks. They have to be, sometimes, to get the job done. However, that does not prevent the growth of humor. Bond together with other employees and find ways to bring more humor into your workplace. For more on how to do this, see Chapter 5, **Humor on the Job.**

7. Do you feel you laugh more when you've had a few drinks?

Ever seen a grown man wear a lamp shade? You have if you've gone to many parties where lots of drinks were served. Alcohol suppresses our inhibitions, and we act silly. However, if we <u>need</u> to have a few drinks to act silly, we are concerning ourselves too much with what other people will think. Alcohol does not create humor; it merely overshadows our fears of peer perception, authority, and self-dignity.

If we laugh more with a few drinks than without, our stress levels far outweigh our humor level. As we learn to laugh more each day, our stress will decrease, while our ability to recognize humor will increase.

8. Do you ever laugh at yourself?

This is one of the most important questions about humor. How we see ourselves influences how other people perceive us. If we feel confident about who we are, that confidence will project; unfortunately, so will our lack of confidence.

Being able to laugh at ourselves means that we are comfortable with who we are. We are not afraid to be laughed at. No one likes to have people point and laugh, but it does happen. Most of the time it is not aimed at us, but at what we are doing, or what we have said.

This is the key to understanding humor. It is easy to make fun of other people and laugh at them, but being able to make people laugh by making fun of ourselves is the key to a strong sense of humor.

Successful humorists all make fun of themselves. It is not all that they do, but it is a part of their presentation. When we make fun of ourselves, we are taking a risk; that takes guts, confidence, and strength. Other people admire that. Making fun of ourselves also lets others know that we don't take ourselves too seriously. If we cannot laugh at ourselves, then we need to lighten up!

9. When embarrassed, do you laugh or get angry?

We all get embarrassed or get caught in awkward situations. That's part of life. But only the confident and the secure can laugh off embarrassment, rather than get upset. We all have had the experience of spilling something or dropping something in the middle of a formal party. Did we turn that situation into a joke so that it diffused the awkwardness? Or did we try to hide or brush off the incident in an effort to cover our embarrassment?

10. Do you enjoy watching children at play?

Watching children is different from supervising children. An opportunity to watch children at play is one of the most entertaining pleasures of life. Children are not bound by our ties to social graces and responsibilities. They act on every impulse.

As we watch children at play, we also learn how to be silly and playful. More important, we can just laugh at what children do and say. Not that we don't take children seriously; but their simple approach and free expression of playfulness make children a valuable resource for humor.

Summary

By examining your answers to the previous questions and by understanding their meanings, you can better understand the importance of humor and how often you can take advantage of its gifts.

However, having a sense of humor and using it appropriately are two very different things. Read on; the following chapters will help you to further develop your laughter skills.

9

How to Find Humor

Humor is truth in an intoxicated condition.
George Jean Nathan

Although humor is easier to attain than riches, humor is far more elusive. Though it is not a winning lottery ticket that you can cash in for millions, it is a treasure which will enrich your life in a million ways. Humor is as easy to find as waking up one morning and saying, "Today I will look on the light side. I will find the laughter in life, not the tears."

However, part of the spontaneity of humor is not to be found by diligently searching for it. We can travel all over the world and have sessions with the great gurus of humor; but if we are not open to it when it appears, we will miss it. Two women were in the checkout line at the grocery store. One said to the other,

> *My daughter thinks she's old enough to make up her own mind and she doesn't even make up her own bed.*

The woman was so busy thinking about her problems with her daughter that she didn't even hear the humor in her own monologue!

Sometimes we forget that we can amuse the world ourselves with some of the things we do. For example, someone once told Lola that if you rub the sticky side of a sheet of stamps over your hair, the stamps can be folded and will never stick together. Lola loves to buy the unusual stamps that only come in sheets. As soon as she purchases them, she turns around and begins rubbing them all over her hair.

She has been doing this so long that she thinks nothing of it. However, the people in the post office stare as she performs this ritual. When Lola looks around and sees the people staring, she grins and says, "Keeps them from sticking," as she walks out the door. The people mumble, "Yeah," "Sure," "Right," and some whisper, "Bonkers."

Luck is largely a matter of paying attention.
-- Susan M. Dodd

Woody Allen says that 70% of success is showing up. We must "show up" for humor. Humor is a sense, much like seeing, hearing, or tasting. Just as some people can figure out the ingredients of a certain recipe by taking just one bite, others can see or hear the humor in a situation immediately.

Stu and Jeanne are members of a civic group who once stayed up all night baking cookies for a fundraising drive. As the night wore on, fatigue was overtaking some of the members. The president related that he had been a guest to dinner at a friend's house where the hostess served a marvelous dessert. "She called it Better Than Sex Cake," related the president. Stu lightened the evening as he quipped, "Must have been a layer cake!"

We consider humorists and comedians to be masters of humor. Their keen sense of the ridiculous gives them the ability to use humor as a tool. Just as master chefs use their innate knowledge to make tasty creations, so too do humorists use their innate sense of the outrageous to make people laugh. **Laughter is the handshake of good communication.**

However, humor is universal, and some people are really in tune to this universality. A good example is Bill Cosby. His humor focuses on family life, both from the viewpoint of a child and from the viewpoint of a parent. His humor reaches a larger audience because of the universality of the theme. We can all relate to childhood and the challenges of parenting. Use the test of universality as you search for humor to aid your writing and speaking.

However, not even Bill Cosby makes everyone laugh. Which brings us back to the challenging of finding humor. Where is it?

Humor is all around us. It can be found in the most unlikely places: in the home, in the office, and in the school. How do we recognize it? Remember, we first have to be willing to FIND it.

Recently, Jeanne needed a gift for a friend. She decided to look in a local gift shop which specialized in spiritual books and gift items; the shop is called "Mystic Moment." After successfully locating an appropriate meditation tape, she took her selection to the girl at the counter. The sales clerk questioned, in what she undoubtedly considered a sincere and spiritual tone, "How did you hear about us?" Equally sincere and spiritual, Jeanne responded: "ESP"!

Once we open ourselves up to the possibility of finding humor, we realize that humor is all based on perception. What we perceive can be either humorous or not. Remember, Webster's defined "humor" as a state of mind. We can choose to be in a humorous state of mind.

If we take a group of people from different walks of life, or even from similar backgrounds, we will find that not everyone in the group will laugh at the same thing or find the same thing humorous. Some need humor to be pointed out to them; others find it on their own. Those who laugh have chosen it by their openness.

However, one of the most exciting things about laughter is that, not unlike chicken pox, it is contagious. Just hearing other people laugh can make us get tickled and enjoy the moment ourselves.

Consider how many times we have been with a group of people and they laughed but we didn't, and yet the sound of their laughter at least made us smile inside.

Consider the number of times we have laughed when no one else did. It happens all the time. Now, just because we did laugh and the others didn't doesn't necessarily mean we don't have a good sense of humor.

There are all kinds of humor--slapstick, sarcastic, cerebral, unapparent, and obvious. What reaches one person and tickles them may leave us totally cold and vice versa.

Slapstick is generally known through sight gags. More often than not, it involves someone either getting hurt or embarrassed, or both. The most common example is someone slipping on a banana peel. Some find this hilarious, while others find it painful. Children's cartoons are rife with examples of slapstick humor. The Roadrunner is always playing tricks which result in Wiley Coyote falling off a cliff or slamming into a mountain.

Sarcasm is humor. We call sarcasm "humor harassment." Sarcasm uses the foibles and weaknesses of others as the tool to produce the humor. This harassment humor is seldom welcome, particularly if we are the targets. Those who use sarcastic humor are bullies, disguising their harassment with phrases such as, "I was only teasing," or "Come on. Can't you take a joke?" Don't walk away from these people--run away from them! They are perverting humor into something painful, and humor is not meant to be painful.

Cerebral humor is generally accomplished with words, either a play on words or a story. The words paint a picture in our heads which is funny. Shakespeare was a master of cerebral humor. Two characters battling with nothing more than words can be very funny.

Consider this example of a conversation between Winston Churchill and Lady Astor.

> *Lady Astor (to Churchill): If you were my husband, I'd poison your coffee.*
>
> *Sir Winston: If you were my wife, I'd drink it.*

Unapparent humor is only for truly attentive and alert people. Lola has a colleague who is a master at unapparent humor. In the middle of a serious discussion, he can interject an observation or make a comment that will never fail to crack everyone up. He always does this with the straightest of faces. Lola admitted that it was years before she was aware that he was doing it. Then, she would start to laugh in the middle of a serious conversation, while he kept that same straight face. That's why they became such good friends. Not everyone understood and appreciated his humor.

Obvious humor is generally anything that can be classified as universally funny. Jokes can be considered obvious humor, even though they may not make us laugh. Although both can be universal, there is a difference between telling jokes and creating humor.

Successful humorists do not rely upon joke-telling. They create humor. Bill Cosby does not tell jokes. Instead, he has us look at everyday situations in a different way. In other words, he alters our perception. This alteration helps us to see the humor in common situations.

Is it funny for someone to be dying of AIDS? Of course not. Can the person who is dying of AIDS be funny? Of course. If the person who is dying chooses to continue to laugh and find the humor in the situation, the act of dying can actually be perceived to be funny. However tragic dying may be, it does not necessarily mean that humor no longer exists. Again, it's all based on perception.

Alcoholism is not considered to be a funny disease, either. Yet, The *Big Book of Alcoholics Anonymous* exhorts the recovering alcoholic to look on the light side and to enjoy the shared humor of situations. Yesterday's tragedy is tomorrow's humor.

When Lola discovered a lump in her breast, she was not convulsed with laughter. However, through the course of diagnosis, breast amputation, and reconstruction, she continued to find the humor in the situation. Six months after the mastectomy, she called her friend, Bruce. She said, "Bruce, this is Lola Gillebaard." There was a long pause. Finally, Bruce said, "Lola, I heard you died." She responded, "Bruce, this is a toll call."

That could have been a very awkward moment, but Lola decided to see the humor in it, and they both laughed. Her cancer has created situations that were funny. Today, she still reflects and laughs. Though cancer took away her breast, it did not take away her sense of humor.

To find humor is easy. Be willing and, the next thing you know, your perception will change. You'll be able to see the humor in even the most tragic of circumstances.

Ten Ways to Get More Humor into Your Life

1. **Adopt the Red Nose Attitude**. In other words, we take our life and our work seriously, but we do not need to take ourselves quite so seriously. We're able to laugh at ourselves, even before anyone else does. Buy a red nose for yourself and for those you love. (This is discussed in more details in Chapter 11, **The Use of Costumes and Props**.) It's a two-dollar investment at any magic shop, and it creates lots of fun. Is it always appropriate to wear a red nose? Of course not. But it is always appropriate to have a red nose attitude!

2. **Create a humor bulletin board at your desk, by the water cooler, on the family refrigerator, or all three.** Encourage everyone you work with and live with to contribute to this humor bulletin board by bringing in their favorite cartoons and funny photographs. Children love to see pictures of their parents looking silly. Employees love to see pictures of their boss looking silly AWAY FROM THE WORKPLACE.

Since Lola is addicted to Post-Its, her favorite cartoon is of a woman sitting at her desk covered with Post-Its, including two on her forehead and several on her blouse. The caption reads, "Some days it seems the only thing holding your life together is sticky notes."

Another favorite pictures a man and woman sitting up in bed looking straight ahead, both wearing big, red noses. The caption reads, "Do you think this is what the therapist meant when she said we should put more fun into our sex life?"

3. **Keep less than charming co-workers from getting to you by visualizing them in humorous situations.**

a. **The Office Gossip:** Every time this person walks toward you, picture them on the cover of the *National Enquirer* with the headline: **"Expose! Local Gossip Sentenced To Solitary Confinement For Foot In Mouth Disease!"**

b. **Prissy Colleague:** As this person comes toward you, picture them without any clothes on.

c. **Obnoxious Client:** Picture them sitting on a tiny high chair at the children's table for Christmas dinner.

4. **Prepare ad-libs for those difficult people in your life whom you cannot avoid.** (If you CAN avoid them, RUN, don't walk, as fast and as far as you can.) If you must be around them, prepare a variety of ad-libs to help to deflect their barbs. For example, if you can expect someone to say, "I really don't like you," a good answer might be, "Are you absolutely sure? Everyone else does."

5. **Think of sincere compliments for difficult people.** Difficult people do not expect to receive compliments. You disarm them when you give them one. Here are two that will always be truthful. "Your phone has a beautiful ring," and "I love the way you clear your throat."

6. **Acquire some audio tapes that you think are funny**. Humor is very personal, so make sure YOU think the tapes are funny. Then PLAY them. Play them on the way to and from work and other places you go in your car. You will laugh in spite of yourself. Once you start to laugh, you will relax, and the stress of the day will be diffused.

7. **Spend the day with a child and don't say a word**. This kid should not be your own because you will not be able to keep your mouth shut. Kids have the sense of fun and play that we all seem to lose when we became a "mature adult" and get a "real job." It's that excitement of being a kid that we're trying to recapture.

If you don't like children, refer to one of the other nine ways.

8. **Remember, laughter is contagious; find a funny friend.** Funny people are all around us in our world. Look for them, and listen to them. Most funny people do not realize that they are funny. Learn from them, and enjoy them.

9. **Be enthusiastic**. Look for people in your life who are doing something right and tell them. Enthusiasm is expressed by speaking louder and faster. Become a cheerleader for life!

    Stu and Jeanne were once in a business which required great enthusiasm during their presentations to new prospects. One of the successful leaders of the group shared his secret for enthusiasm with them. Before each presentation, he would stand in a corner and cluck like a chicken. Although that may sound ridiculous, try it. It's hard to be blase while clucking like a chicken and flapping your arms around like chicken wings!

10. **Perfect your smile and a positive attitude**. If you don't feel like it, fake it! People won't know you're faking it, and they will give both the smile and the positive attitude back to you. Before you know it, you're not faking it any more--it's real!

10

Humor and Speaking

It takes a lot of practice to get spontaneous.
-- Anonymous

In today's world a person must be able to communicate effectively to succeed. The ability to convincingly use communication skills is a major determinant in who becomes President of the United States, or U.S. Senator, or chairman of the board.

However, speaking with humor is crucial, even in a phone booth. Whether you need to present a report to the PTA or complain to the board of directors of your homeowner's association or have coffee with a new friend or business prospect, you are getting ready for a public speech. Each of these examples of communication situations, as well as most others, are great opportunities for using humor in speaking.

Our world's history has been guided by those who have mastered the art of communication. Pericles, Demosthenes, Cicero, and Cato were major orators in classical times. The speeches of Thomas Jefferson, Daniel Webster, Abraham

Lincoln, and Susan B. Anthony played a major role in the development of our nation. John F. Kennedy, Martin Luther King, Jr., and Ronald Reagan influenced our recent history. Each one of these individuals displayed an ability to communicate coherently, effectively, and persuasively; and each knew when to inject humor for that relaxing laughter break.

These shapers of history are examples of the power of public speaking. They have presented new and revolutionary ideas, primarily through the spoken word. Each used oral language as their primary method of communicating their ideas to large numbers of people. This high degree of effectiveness in public speaking is not impossible to achieve. To present our ideas and messages, we merely need to follow a few guidelines.

First, public speaking is generally an uninterrupted speech. Therefore, it is not casual like a conversation. In a speech, we are addressing a group of many individuals. Our goal is to communicate our views, opinions, and ideas.

This is true for any type of speaking, including comedy. Our audiences will not laugh if we fail to effectively express ourselves. We need to speak clearly so that our words can be understood. Timing is the key to the delivery of humorous material. Pauses should be used to ensure that the audience has time to find the humor in our material.

Second, public speaking is better organized than conversation. Organization is important for all types of presentations. If a humorist does not set up a story properly, the audience will not laugh at the right time. The best humorists build up to a point. In a sense, the humorist starts a fire and keeps fueling the fire until it becomes a roaring blaze.

Laughter must be cultivated in a similar fashion. One rule is absolute in speaking: Never talk during a laugh; you will throw away lines that no one will hear.

Third, public speaking requires very defined nonverbal behavior. In Chapter 11 we talk about the use of props and how they can also be a distraction. So, too, can our body movement distract the audience, taking away from the content of our speech. If we are moving frantically across the platform, we will come across as nervous. Throwing our arms about will overshadow our message.

For a serious presentation, we should use minimal arm movement, stand straight, and not feel as if we have to move. This gives more emphasis to our content.

In humorous presentations we use our bodies to amplify the humor of our talk. The more subtle the form of humor we are using, the more subtle our movements should be. Let the content dictate the movement. Robin Williams uses every part of his body for humor, from the swaying of his arms to the swoosh of his tush.

Bob Newhart, on the other hand, uses minimal movement, but a simple raise of his eyebrows is very effective.

An important aspect to remember about public speaking is that we are either providing people with information or are trying to change attitudes or behavior. Humor can help to give our presentations more spark in either case. The idea is to educate our audiences while keeping them awake. Using a few choice pieces of humor during our presentations will give our audiences a comedy break.

This is especially effective when there is much material to be covered. There is no real difference between the attention span of a child and that of an adult. Children just haven't learned how to act "as if" they are listening.

By interjecting levity at the right moments we will recapture the attention of our audience without distracting from our message. Humor allows our audience to laugh, alleviating stress and boredom and giving our speech more strength. Humor alone does not make our speech better, but it does create a positive emotional bond with the audience. Humor is as effective in public speaking as the use of props. If not properly used, it can be just as distracting.

If we are covering a great many new ideas or concepts in our presentation, the eyes of our audience could glaze over at any moment. They begin to think about what we've said, and that thinking prevents them from focusing on what we are saying at the moment.

The rule of thumb is to inject humor every eight minutes. The laughter energizes our audience and they are once again ready to concentrate on what we have to say.

Humor is also an excellent tool in a persuasive presentation. Members of our audience will have preconceived ideas and we must influence those preconceptions. Humor relaxes the audience, making them comfortable and creating an atmosphere more receptive to our ideas.

We are always competing for the attention of our audience. If the presentation goes too long without humor breaks, people will begin to think about phone calls they need to make, or how to finish that proposal they are working on. The audience was not created the day of our presentation; they have lives outside of our program.

Why is it that listeners always know when the speaker should stop and he seldom does?

-- Malcolm Forbes

This may sound obvious and silly, but many speakers forget that many people in the audience may have had a very bad day, so far, or maybe several are looking forward to an exciting date, or an old friend is coming to town. Many may have financial problems which may be worrying their thoughts. We, as the speakers, are competing with all this internal noise.

Humor can be our best weapon against conflicting internal noise in the heads of our audience. The whole world likes to laugh, and, of course, when people are laughing and having a good time, they forget their problems. By injecting relevant humor every eight minutes, we not only make the speech more entertaining, but we allow our audience to settle back, forget their own troubles, and enjoy our speech.

How then do we inject humor into our presentations? First, we look within our own subject matter for ironies and situations which can be exaggerated to be made funny. Humor which arises out of the text is very effective with an audience.

In addition, we can research humorous anecdotes and quotations in the library. *Toastmasters* has published several resource books which contain humorous material. There are numerous speaker's resource books which can provide more material.

We need to become collectors of humorous stories and quotations. We can find them when reading about our subject, in the newspapers and trade periodicals, and in many other printed materials. We should develop a personal file of humorous material which we label with topical references which are easily understood. Creating computer databases of humor is an excellent approach.

Always avoid telling your audience that you are going to tell them something humorous. If you say, "I'm going to tell you a joke . . ." and no one laughs, you'll be the one with egg all over your face. This is one of the hardest situations from which a speaker has to recover. You can prevent it from happening in the first place. Simply tell the story; the audience response will determine whether or not it was a joke.

Trying out humorous material in front of family or friends before using it in a public speaking situation is always a good idea. When we deliver humorous stories or quotations cold, we may not get any reaction or at least not the reaction we were hoping for. A few polite groans may not be what we had in mind. Rehearsing the material will give us opportunities to improve on the delivery and the timing, two elements which are crucial to success in using humorous material.

Many professional speakers seek the services of a "coach." If you plan to do a lot of public speaking, this is an excellent idea. Search until you find someone with good academic credentials and experience in working on humor in public speaking. A good coach can improve your general public speaking skills and work with you on the humorous aspects of your presentation. Although some cost is involved, it will be well worth it.

If you are financially unable to hire a professional coach, you may want to join Toastmasters or take a public speaking class through an adult school, college, or university in your area. Again, try to find a program where you both learn about humorous speaking and practice and refine your own humorous speaking skills.

Although there is no sure way to guarantee a receptive audience, the first step is to organize your ideas and keep your presentation coherent and concise. Humor can always be used to entice the audience long enough for you to convey your message. Humor is the competitive edge in delivering a successful presentation. This edge will open doors for you and pave the way for a more rewarding and enjoyable career.

Exercises to Tickle the Funnybone

1. Choose a personal story from your life. Tell that story to the next person or persons with whom you feel comfortable (best not a member of your family because they'll argue with you about how it REALLY happened!). When you tell the story, be sure to listen to it yourself and pay attention to where the people laugh. One important element of humor is exaggeration, so you might want to exaggerate the funniest parts.

2. Continue to practice your story with friends and strangers, but NEVER NEVER tell them what you are doing. Just listen to their reaction. If they say, "What I thought you were going to say was . . ." listen to

that. It's probably funnier than what you said, so use it. The other reaction you might get is, "Wouldn't it be funnier if . . .?" Listen to that and see if you can incorporate it in your story.

3. At your favorite supermarket, get into the longest checkout line on purpose. Then, watch and listen to the people in the line. People say and do the funniest things without even intending to. You can find humor as well as examples for your speeches and writings.

Jeanne overheard a man discussing his illness with someone: "I've got shingles," said the man. "That's terrible," replied his friend. "Is it very painful?" "Only when they nail them on," cracked the sufferer.

Listen to the humor happening around you!

11

The Use of Costumes and Props

Humor is grown-up play.
-- Max Eastman

Since the beginning of mankind, props have been an effective tool in communicating, be it a stick to draw figures in the sand or more sophisticated tools.

The early Greeks relied upon props on stage to define character changes. They spent little time, if any, on sets. Actors would change their dress and their props and the scene would immediately become different. To them, the prop was an essential ingredient for a successful play.

Imagine how difficult it would be to explain a jet plane to a native of a foreign island who had never seen or heard a plane. A diagram or picture helps the audience to better visualize what you are describing. Props can also help to establish connections between different languages and cultures. In fact, it is the naming of objects that established the beginnings of language.

Visual aids are crucial to proper communication. It's true that a picture is worth a
thousand words. Research has shown that
people learn considerably more when ideas
appeal to the eye as well as to the ear.

Our presentations can be more effective
when they include a visual aid or a prop to further illustrate our ideas. However, props should
never be a crutch and must not be relied upon
as the sole form of communication. They should
be used only to emphasize a point.

The only prop that Lola uses in her workshops and seminars is a big red nose. She puts
it on to emphasize to the audience that we all
should have the "red nose attitude." She uses
the nose to also loosen up her own comic juices
whenever she is feeling dry. If she feels that she
is taking life too seriously, she puts her red nose
in her pocket and goes to a neighborhood grocery store. She picks up a couple of items and
then stands in the longest line she can find.

She slips the red nose on and starts to read a
magazine. She's always amazed at how people
react. Mothers clutch their children to them and
make them look away. Some people talk to her
as if absolutely nothing is different. Others
laugh.

Children are always the best. A kid will walk
up to her and stare and ask, "Why are you
wearing that nose?" Lola will answer, "To protect
my other one." Children think that's a fine
answer.

The comedian Gallagher is a great believer in props. Although he is very humorous without visual aids, his love of props becomes a wonderful treat to watch. His imagination truly comes alive on stage. He's famous for his "Sludge-O-Matic" routine, which is nothing more than a sledge hammer squashing fruits and vegetables. Gallagher has truly mastered the use of visual aids.

And that's exactly what props are to be used for--a visual aid.

We must be careful not to clutter the stage with too many props or our audience will lose the ideas we are trying to present amidst all the visual stimulation. Keep your props simple, and remember that using too many will take away from the presentation.

Once Lola was conveying an idea about snakes. While making her presentation, she had a boa-constrictor wrapped around her body. The idea was to gain the audience's attention. Unfortunately, it instead created a feeling of panic. It never occurred to Lola that many people do not like snakes. Their panic made it impossible for them to enjoy her presentation. True, the audience did not forget the snake, but they also missed most of the points that Lola wanted them to remember. In this all-too-true example, the prop that was intended to be a visual aid had, instead, become a distraction.

It is important that we think carefully about our props and always ask ourselves, "Are these really necessary?"

George Burns is a perfect example of some-one who uses a prop to perfection. He presents his delightful humor with one hand in his pocket and with the other holding his cigar. When the audience laughs at a joke, he puffs his cigar. He never smokes, he just puffs. The cigar is a crucial part of his timing. He would never do a comedy routine without one.

Sometimes, unplanned circumstances pro-vide us with opportunities and props. Once, when Lola spoke at a nurse's convention, the theme for the gathering was *The Wizard of Oz*. A yellow brick road adorned the floor. The song of the same name blared from the sound system. The Lion, the Tin Man, the Scarecrow, and Dorothy skipped through the audience laughing and talking with the crowd.

All 500 people in the audience wore red sequined slippers just like Dorothy's. Toes were "twinkling" throughout the room as Lola was being introduced. Before she said a word, she just stared at the audience. They stared back. Several seconds passed. And then Lola yelled, "Auntie Em! Auntie Em!" The audience laughed and cheered. Lola had taken advantage of the props at hand and had used them to bond with her audience.

On another occasion, Lola was speaking to fourteen hundred members of the Beta Sigma Phi sorority. Before she went on, she noticed that the sorority members called each other "sister." She had also noticed that every car in the parking lot had a Beta Sigma Phi license plate. And then she overheard a sorority sister talking to a sorority board member:

Sister: Those white outfits you board members are wearing are just beautiful.

Board member: Thank you. You know what we call ourselves, don't you?

Sister: No, what?

Board member: Born-again Virgins.

So Lola opened her program with a loud "Good Morning, Sisters." They roared back, "Good Morning." And then Lola told about noticing the license plates and being impressed with the passion these people showed for the sorority. With that, she told what she had overheard between the sister and the board member. The crowd roared again. Lola had shown them that she knew what they cared about. She did this by looking and listening and using what she saw and heard for a prop. So, look, listen, and acknowledge. We can often take advantage of what is going on around us.

Thus far, we have talked primarily about the use of props in speaking situations. However, props can also make us more effective in doing our day-to-day jobs.

Everyone who works sometimes has to relieve the stress of their job with humor. Classroom teachers frequently need to "lighten up" or lose their students. Using only those things normally found in a school room, they create props which can be very humorous.

One teacher cut out cartoons from the newspapers. On a duplicating machine she enlarged them and then made overhead transparencies. Whenever things needed livening in her classroom, she would toss one of the cartoons on the overhead projector and give her students a humor break. Many professional speakers use cartoons projected on an overhead as a way to get into their presentation.

Costume dressing is a regular event at the hair saloon which Jeanne patronizes. The husband and wife who own the shop declare certain days as "dress up" days for special occasions. Patrons enjoy the atmosphere for Christmas, Halloween, and other holidays. Some make sure to book appointments for those special days so that they can enjoy the day, too.

If you've never thought of a dentist as a particularly humorous professional, then you've never visited one we were told about. This ingenuous fellow recognized the need to distract his patients and relieve their nervousness. So, he invested in a few simple props to provide a lighter touch to a normally frightening experience for many. With false moustaches and beards, outsize glasses, and phony ears, he caused patients to laugh and thus created an atmosphere where he could help more patients. He also told jokes while working in a patient's mouth.

Many of us have been driving down the street and spotted a figure in a clown costume on the corner. Usually a new business is announcing its opening or an old, established one is having a special sale. In either case, the business owner recognizes the drawing ability of a clown figure.

Some important rules to remember about visual aids:

1. Show visual aids only when you are talking about them. When you are using a visual aid, direct the attention of the audience to it. When you are finished using it, remove it immediately. Otherwise, it can become a distraction.

2. Show the visual aid so that the entire audience can see it. If you hold it, be sure to hold it our away from your body and move it about slowly so that the entire audience can see it. Nothing will distract and irritate an audience more than not being able to see a prop.

3. Your visual aid does not have ears. Therefore, do not talk to the prop while displaying it. It is important for you to talk to the audience when using the prop in order to

keep your message focused and understood. Nothing kills a humorous bit faster
than garbled words.

4. Keep it simple. Do not overdo the use of
    props. Remember, props are a form of
    emphasis, but emphasizing too many
    points results in no emphasis at all. Too
    many props will overwhelm your audience
    and lose their attention.

Exercises to Tickle the Funny Bone

1. This exercise teaches how to really have
    fun when you're eating out alone. The prop
    you carry with you is a book, preferably
    one you are not interested in because you
    will not read it. Ask for a table or booth in
    a crowded area. Sit down and open your
    book. Stare at the page and even turn it
    once in a while, but what you're really
    doing is listening to the dialogue of the
    people around you.

    You will not only hear things that will
    make you laugh; you will hear things that,
    if you made them up, you would not
    believe. Write these funny things down in
    a notebook as if you were taking notes
    from the book. You can use this material
    in speaking and writing.

2. Invest in a foam red nose. Carry it with
    you wherever you go. Slip it on when
    you're in bumper-to-bumper traffic. You'll

be amazed at how many people will keep coming up beside you to see if they saw what they think they saw.

3. Wear a shower cap to the dinner table and see how long it takes for someone to notice it and make a comment.

4. Invest in a walking stick for fun and see how many different ways you can use it, e.g., a pointer, a baton, an exercise bar, etc.

12

Writing Funny

You can be on the right road, but you gotta keep moving or you'll get run over.

-- *Will Rogers*

Writing the Serious/Humorous Article

We sit down to write about something. We don't sit down to write something funny. The humor punches up the serious as we move along. As we look through the various types of magazine markets in *The Writer's Market*, we are amazed at the number of times "humor" is listed as a sought-after category.

For years, Lola has been creating and selling "humor pieces." In looking through these published pieces, Lola discovered that they seemed to fall into three categories. The first is the basically serious piece which is made more palatable by some occasional levity--a humorous twist to a sentence, a wry observation, a felicitous arrangement of words that produces a humorous effect.

Several years ago Lola was asked to write an article about relationships and to comment on her 30-year marriage to the same man. Obviously, Lola's "comment" article would be serious, but she decided she wanted to engage the reader immediately, and she chose to do it with a humorous opening "hook." Her first line was, "It was in 1954 that he and I moved the site of our relationship from the back seat of his car to our own apartment."

This mildly humorous opening said to the reader, "There will be some serious things in this article, but the author does not take herself or her opinions too seriously. She's a balanced person with some sense of humor and perspective--no fanatic."

Another example of using humor to lighten a basically serious piece was an article which Lola wrote for the *Conservative Digest* which began, "I've just written my congressman urging him to support ERP--Equal Rights For Parents." She continues:

My husband Hank and I believe in sharing, as do our four sons. Their philosophy of sharing is simple: "What's yours is ours and what's ours is ours alone." What followed was a serious piece about kids and selfishness, but the humor perspective always showed.

The second type of humorous-serious piece is the article which, while still making a serious point, has more than just a touch of humor. The general tone of such an article is lighthearted and recounts humorous incidents to drive home its basic serious message.

For centuries, satirists have used humor to point up social injustices or to poke fun at the society which was taking itself too seriously. Satire is a very subtle form of humor and requires a light touch on the part of the writer. Nothing seems more contrived and less artless than satire which is purposely trying to be funny.

Satire's chief ingredient is exaggeration. When we take a serious political or societal problem and exaggerate it, we can see its ridiculousness. Those who wish to write satire would be well served to read Art Buchwald and others who specialize in this type of humor.

Then there's the totally humorous article, written "just to be funny," with really no serious point at all. This is probably the hardest type of humor piece to write, because maintaining consistent humor without posturing or straining is very difficult.

Lola sold one such piece which was entitled "The Weirdly Unaverage American." This article poked fun at a book that had been published earlier, called The Average American. Lola laughed at the listed statistics in the book that covered everything from sex to garbage cans.

Her ending quotes a question from the book: "Do you think that a one-child family is a good idea?" Her answer reads, "I definitely do, but I already had four sons when I decided this."

As James Kilpatrick says in his book, *The Writer's Art*, "'Writing funny' is the toughest of all areas of popular writing . . . The writer who has the gift of laughter, and puts that gift on paper, can write his or her own ticket."

Exercises to Tickle the Funny Bone

1. Collect 20 jokes that you think are funny. They can come from any source you choose. Remember, you must like them. Next type or print these jokes on a piece of paper and analyze them. List next to each of them what you think makes them funny. Do you laugh because of the words, or is it the image the words evoke in your head? This exercise will not only give you a great collection of good jokes; it will also help you to understand your own likes and dislikes so that you can generate your own style of writing.

2. Collect at least 20 unusual photos. Remember, the crazier the picture, the better. Now write humorous captions for the photos. Try to create new meaning for the photos, not just settling for what is obvious. Maybe it's a photo of your family standing in the yard talking. Maybe in the photo all seven members have their

mouths open. The caption might be, "I hate it when Mom makes us go on this fly diet."

3. Collect 24 cartoons that you especially like. Recaption the cartoons with lines of your own. Don't limit yourself. Do several for each cartoon. Remember, no matter how great the cartoon is, there's no guarantee that the caption already on it is the best one that can be written. This exercise also teaches you not to quit too soon.

4. For a study in humor and rhythm, come up with your own version of the following:

   "Old soldiers never die. They just fade away."

   Examples:

   "Old teachers never die, they just lose their class."

   "Old lumberjacks never die, they just drop their trunks."

5. Gene Perret, in his book, *Comedy Writing Workbook*, suggests that you make two lists of ten nouns. Make them as bizarre and zany as you want. (It's also fun to get someone else to make the list for you.) Then, take the first noun from column one and the first noun from column two.

Combine these two words into some kind of funny line.

Examples:

Death/Varnish: My great aunt died when she accidentally swallowed a can of varnish, but everyone said she had a lovely finish.

Peanut Butter/Whale: If you're ever swallowed by a whale, cover yourself with peanut butter and you can at least stick to the roof of his mouth.

13

The Proactive Humorist:

Putting It All Together

So . . . . now that you've read the book and decided that maybe you ought to put some humor into your life, what do you do next? The first step is to clarify your goals and objectives in using humor. There is a wealth of difference between the person who wants to diffuse family stress with humor and the person who wants to improve his/her speaking style with jokes and cartoons.

You are the only one who can make the important decision as to what you want to do with humor. Take a few minutes to jot down some areas which you would like to work on. A sample list might look something like this:

1. Make holiday dinners bearable. They're so stressful now that everyone gets indigestion just thinking about them.

2. Reduce the stress on the job. Tension is making it difficult to accomplish the day-to-day tasks.

3. Improve your personal health through humor. Take steps to develop better coping skills by looking on the lighter side of life.

By the way, if one or more of the items on the list sounds familiar, don't be surprised. These are the kinds of issues that most of us face.

Now that you have your list, select the area that you would like to work on first. Don't try to solve all of them at once or the task my seem too overwhelming. In making your selection, you may want to tackle the one which seems easiest to you first. Success in this area will give you the confidence to move into the more challenging areas.

On the other hand, if there is a situation which is really driving you bonkers, it may need immediate attention. Whatever the reason for your choice, there is no wrong way to choose. The only way to lose in this situation is not to start at all.

Developing a plan of action is the next step in instilling more humor into your life. Review the appropriate chapter(s) first, paying particular attention to the "Exercises to Tickle Your Funny Bone." You may want to make notes of ideas you really like. Brainstorm some other ideas which you can add to those in the book.

You may want to consult another resource. We have listed several, including books, references, and individuals who are available for specific coaching and consulting. After you have what appears to be a fairly complete list, sequence the items in whatever order makes sense to you.

Action is now called for. If your goals are personal, you may want to enlist the support of significant others in your life. If your goals are professional, the services of a professional coach can be beneficial. You may want to join a self-help group or enroll in a class at a local college or adult school program. All of these steps are beneficial to your well-being because you are moving in a positive and constructive manner toward improving your life.

Remember, instilling more humor into your life involves some risk taking. For example, Stu is regarded as something of a punster. However, not all of his puns are considered funny by his listeners. You need to be willing to risk the negative reaction of those about you. Because humor is in the eye and ear of the beholder, your audience may not find your attempts very funny. Don't give up! Everyone who uses humor finds a personal style through trial and error.

If you are attempting to use humor in speaking and writing, a supportive personal group should be found. Try out your initial efforts on them before going public. Humor in speaking needs to be practiced in order to develop good timing. *Toastmasters* is an excellent place for the fledgling speaker to practice and develop.

Humor in writing can be even more challenging, since the writer has only the printed word by which to transmit his thoughts and feelings. Showcase your efforts with your support group first to find out what works and what doesn't.

Become your own clipping service. Whenever you read, whether it's newspapers, books, or magazines, be on the lookout for material you can use. Make a collection of cartoons, quotations, quips, jokes, etc., which you can adapt and use. One personal use of this material could be to design your own greeting cards. An immediate business use could be to include short quips and quotations in memos and bulletins where appropriate.

Remember, nothing falls flatter than inappropriate humor. If one single person is offended by your efforts, then you cannot really consider your humor to be successful. This is where your support group can come in handy. Ask them to listen or read your material, looking for things that might be offensive because of racial, ethnic, sex or gender, or any other reference. It is better to err on the side of propriety than to risk looking like a fool.

Becoming an effective humorist is a lifetime occupation. Whatever aspect of your life you choose to improve with humor is probably a similar situation. It takes continual effort to reduce tension through humor in the family or on the job. However, the effort is worth it in the improvement in personal relations, health, job productivity, etc. Humor is a way that each and every one of us can touch others' lives in a meaningful way.

The authors sincerely hope that you have enjoyed the book and found a way to impact your life with humor. Each of us has survived stressful situations and made a difference in our lives by looking on the lighter side. It is our hope that you will, too!

APPENDIX

Selected Resources

Selected Humor Consultants

Boyd Seminars, 12555 Euclid Street, Suite 25, Garden Grove, CA 92640, (714) 636-5457. **Lorrie Boyd**, DCH, MS, CLP, is a Doctor of Clinical Hypnotherapy and a Certified Leisure Professional who conducts continuing education training programs. Her programs include: "Stress Management, Energy Enhancement, and Performance," "When Life Gives Your Raspberries . . . How to Cope with Grief, Loss, and Change," "How to Develop a Winning Spirit Through Team-Building," & "Humor, Hypnotherapy, and Healing."

Lerner and Associates, 839 E. Davidson Court, Brea, CA 92621, (714) 671-0202. **Stewart Lerner** is a management consultant and trainer who uses humor to defuse emotionally laden personnel issues. Stu's ability to present even complex material in a non-legalistic, easy-to-understand and enjoyable manner has made him a sought-after seminar speaker. His programs include: "Sexual Harrassment/The Kiss of Death," "Termination without Aggravation," and "Perils of the Small Employer." **Jeanne Lerner** is a national champion speaker and speech coach, as well as a mentor/teacher who uses humor to motivate her students as they learn and grow. She is available for groups and one-on-one training in speaking and writing.

Laugh and Learn with Lola, 22191 Paso del Sur, Laguna Beach, CA 92677, (714) 499-1968, FAX (714) 499-9870. **Lola D. Gillebaard** is a humor therapist who specializes in keynotes and training workshops for medical associations, convention kick-offs, and trade show finales. Some of her more popular programs are: "Humor in Business is Serious Business," "Lighten Up Your Sales Presentation to Fatten Up Your Paycheck," "Laughter is the Handshake of Good Communication," and "How to Eat with Your Children Without Throwing Up!"

General Humor

Allen, Steve. *How to Be Funny.* McGraw-Hill, 1987.

Lots of tips on how to discover the comic in you.

Blakely, James ("Doc"). *Push Button Wit.* Rich, 1986.

Indexed by subject, with funny stories on each.

Carter, Judy. *Stand-up Comedy.* Dell, 1989.

How to turn your anxieties into a killer act.

Perret, Gene and Linda. *Gene Perret's Funny Business.* Prentice-Hall, 1990.

Lots of good one-liners related to various businesses and professions.

Robertson, Jeanne. *Humor, the Magic of Genie.* Rich, 1990.

Seven "potions" for developing a sense of humor.

Saks, Sol. *The Craft of Comedy Writing.* Writer's Digest Books, 1985.

Outlines pitfalls of comedy writing, how to avoid them.

Grief/Healing

Buscaglia, Leo. *The Fall of Freddie the Leaf.* Charles B. Stack, Inc., 1982.

An inspiring story for children and adults which illustrates the delicate balance of life and death.

Capacchione, Lucia. *The Well-being Journal.* Newcastle Publishing, 1989.

Provides extensive activities utilizing art therapy, visualizations, and reflective writing for health and well-being.

Colgrove, Melba, Harold Bloomfield, and Peter McWilliams. *How to Survive the Loss of a Love.* Bantam Books, 1976.

Unique, easy-to-apply guide to cope with grief and loss.

Hageseth, Christian. *A Laughing Place: The Art and Psychology of Positive Humor in Love and Adversity.* Berwick, 1988.

An informal, easy-to-read book about humor, life, stress, love, and adversity. Includes a section on humor and grief, and techniques to apply humor into daily life.

Johnson, S. *After a Child Dies: Counseling Bereaved Families.* Springer, 1987.

An excellent resource book with techniques to help families cope with death. Includes an extensive chapter on therapeutic interventions which include humor, storytelling, drawing, dolls, grave visits, and puppetry.

Klein, Allen. *The Healing Power of Humor.* Jeremy P. Tarcher, Inc., 1989.

Specifically focuses on humor and loss. Includes finding laughter in loss and ways to celebrate loss.

Kushner, Harold. *When Bad Things Happen to Good People.* Avon Books, 1981.

An inspiring book about grief, hope, and God.

Rogers, Dale Evans. *Angel Unaware.* A Jove Book, 1963.

A touching story of how Roy Rogers' family was transformed by the short life of their daughter, Robin Elizabeth.

Staudacher, Carol. *Beyond Grief.* New Harbinger Publications, Inc., 1987.

A comprehensive guide for recovering from the death of a loved one.

Business

Belasco, James A. *The Excellent Choice*. Management Development Associates, 1986.

How people create excellence.

Blanchard, Kenneth, and Spencer Johnson. *The One-Minute Manager*. William Morrow & Co., 1981.

Reminds us to take a minute out of our day to look into the faces of the people we manage and to realize that they are our most important assets.

Deming, W. Edwards. *Out of the Crisis*. MIT Center for Advanced Engineering Study, 1982.

Shows America's managers what must be done in order to regain America's competitive position in international commerce.

Naisbitt, John, and Patricia Aburdene. *Re-inventing the Corporation*. Warner Books, 1985.

Explains why the time is ripe to translate personal values into institutional change and corporate policy.

Peters, Tom. *Thriving on Chaos*. Knopf, 1988.

A comprehensive program for revamping American management.

Peters, Tom, and Nancy Austin. *A Passion for Excellence*. Random House, 1985.

Zeroes in on the three key areas of competence that determine the long-term excellence of any organization.

Weisinger, Dr. Hendrie, and Norman M. Lobsenz. *Nobody's Perfect*. Warner Books, 1981.

Learn how to give criticism effectively and to take criticism constructively.

Lifestyle/Personal Growth

Buscaglia, Leo. *Loving Each Other*. Holt, Rinehart & Winston, 1984.

Addresses intricacies and challenges of relationships.

Buscaglia, Leo. *Bus 9 to Paradise*. Slack, 1986.

How existence becomes paradise for those who love many things with a passion.

Covey, Steven. *The 7 Habits of Highly Effective People*. Simon and Schuster, 1989.

Fundamental principles of human effectiveness.

Dyer, Wayne. *Pull Your Own Strings*. Avon, 1977.

How to rid yourself of self-defeating behavior and begin to take charge of your life.

Gawain, Shakti. *Creative Visualization*. Whatever Publishing, 1978.

The art of using mental imagery and affirmation to improve your life.

Hill, Napoleon, and W. Clement Stone. *Success Through Positive Mental Attitude*. Simon and Schuster, 1960.

How to use PMA to set your sights on a goal and attain it through persistent thinking and positive action.

Jampolsky, Gerald. *Teach Only Love*. Bantam, 1983.

Explores the healing power of love and the seven principles of attitudinal healing.

Maltz, Max. *Psycho-cybernetics*. Prentice-Hall, 1960.

Use Self-Image Psychology to create a totally new image of yourself.

Newman, James. *Release Your Brakes*. Warner, 1977.

How to take charge of your life.

Peck, M. Scott (MD). *The Road Less Travelled*. Simon and Schuster, 1978.

How to embrace reality and achieve serenity and fullness in your life.

Robbins, Anthony. *Unlimited Power*. Fawcett, 1986.

Shows how to harness your mind power.

Schwartz, David. *The Magic of Thinking Big*. Prentice-Hall, 1959.

Discover how your thinking makes magic for you.

Siegel, Bernie S. (MD). *Love, Medicine, and Miracles*. Harper and Row, 1988.

Shares lessons learned about self-healing and the power of unconditional love.

Von Oech, Roger. *A Whack on the Side of the Head*. Warner, 1983.

How to unlock your mind for innovation.

Waitley, Denis. *Psychology of Winning*. Nightingale-Conant, 1979.

Teaches formulae for developing the 10 qualities of a total winner.

Waitley, Denis. *Seeds of Greatness*. Revell, 1983.

How to combine positive attitudes with your natural aptitudes or attitudes.

Waitley, Denis. *The Double Win*. Revell, 1985.

Emphasizes that success must be a two-way street.

Speaking/Writing

Dutton, John L. *How to Be an Outstanding Speaker.* Life Skills Publishing, 1986.

Comprehensive step-by-step techniques on how to be a better speaker than 90% of the people you know.

Leech, Thomas. *How to Prepare, Stage, and Deliver Winning Presentations.* Amacom, 1982.

Learn how to improve your presentations.

Malouf, Doug. *How to Create and Deliver a Dynamic Presentation.* Simon and Schuster, 1988.

Helps you to convey your message with the strongest possible impact.

Plotnik, Arthur. *The Elements of Editing.* MacMillan, 1982.

A primer of editing advice.

Ryckman, W. G. *The Art of Speaking Effectively.* Dow Jones-Irwin, 1983.

A personal learning aid to better speaking.

Shertzer, Margaret. *The Elements of Grammar.* MacMillan, 1986.

An authoritative guide to good grammar for writing and speaking.

Simmons, S. H. *New Speaker's Handbook.* Dial, 1972.

How to be the life of the podium and put life into your presentations.

Strunk, William Jr., and E. B. White. *The Elements of Style.* MacMillan Publishing, 1979.

An important companion for anyone who writes.

Newsletters and Catalogues

Laughter Works Warehouse and Newsletter
Publisher: Jim Pelly (1-800-626-LAFF)

Gene Perret's Round Table Comedy Newsletter
Publisher: Linda Perret (1-818-796-4823)

The Laugh Connection (Newsletter)
Publisher: Bob Ross (1-619-479-3331)

Funny Business (Newsletter)
Publisher: Dale Irwin (1-708-852-7695)

Humor Resources Catalogue
Joel Goodman, President (1-518-587-8770); contains books, audiotapes, videotapes, games, and props.

The Whole Mirth Catalogue
Published by Allen Klein, 1034 Page St., San Francisco, CA 94117; lots of fun props, gag gifts, items to make you and those around you laugh.

Order Form

Lerner and Associates
839 E. Davidson Court
Brea, CA 92621

Name: _____

Street: _____

City: _____

State: _____ Zip Code _____

Please send _____ copies of
Change Your Life with Humor
@ $14.95   _____

California Residents:
Please add $1.15 <u>per book</u>
for sales tax   _____

Shipping and Handling:
$3.00 for first book,
plus $1.00 for each
additional book   _____

Total:
(Make check payable to:
Lerner and Associates   _____